A Bird in the Deep
The True Story of the USS Partridge

by James Krouse

A Bird in the Deep

The True Story of the USS Partridge

by James Krouse

Cover Design: James Dziemianzuk

Author Photo: Janet Century

ISBN – 9781626130753

Library of Congress Control Number – 2017933790

Published by ATBOSH Media ltd.

Cleveland, Ohio, USA

http://www.atbosh.com

"A ship at sea is a different world in herself, and in consideration of the protracted and distant operations of the fleet units, the Navy must place great power, responsibility, and trust in the hands of those leaders chosen for command."

Joseph Conrad,
Command at Sea: The Prestige,
Privilege and Burden of Command

Table of Contents

Prologue:
    Superman and the Whale   7

Chapter 1:
    The Bird Boats   15

Chapter 2:
    Lieutenant Wouk's Memo   29

Chapter 3:
    War in Paradise   49

Chapter 4:
    Inheriting *Caine*   85

Chapter 5:
    The New Captain   91

Chapter 6:
    Crossing Over   109

Chapter 7:
    Captain Bligh Stories   123

Chapter 8:
    Mulberries & Whales   135

Chapter 9:
    The Navy Man and Tug Boat Captain   157

Chapter 10:
    Collision At Sea   173

Chapter 11:
    Standing at the Door   187

Chapter 12:
    Lt. Commander Janeway's Investigation   203

Chapter 13:
    The Owl and Captain White   217

Chapter 14:
    Our Whole World   227

Chapter 15:
    Measure of War   245

Chapter 16:
    Strawberries and Ball Bearings   255

Chapter 17:
    Two Ships   261

Chapter 18:
    The Captain's Wife   265

Afterward   275

Acknowledgments   285

About the Author   287

Prologue:
Superman and the Whale

On June 12, 1944, the HMRT *Superman,* a Royal Navy rescue tug, plied the dark waters of the English Channel. The tug was barely a mile off Omaha Beach, where the fighting was still heavy a week after Allied forces landed there in an epic battle for Europe known as D-Day. The tug, built in 1933 as a private vessel, was requisitioned by the British admiralty in 1939 and was now part of Task Force 128, a hodgepodge flotilla of civilian and military craft with a mission so daunting not even the German High Command considered it a realistic threat. Task Force 128 was to create an artificial harbor off the beaches of Normandy. *Superman's* mission orders, taken from the task force war diary, reveal the challenges:

> *Task Force 128 will install GOOSEBERRY No. 1 off Beach UTAH and MULBERRY "A" and GOOSEBERRY No. 2 off Beach OMAHA in order to provide shelter for small craft at both beaches by D plus 2 and insure delivery of 5000 tons of stores per day over beach OMAHA during severe sea and weather conditions after MULBERRY is completed, approximately D plus 18.*

Gooseberry was the codename for the line of sunken ships that would create a break wall to protect the beaches. Mulberry was the codename for a series of pontoon roadways and sunken caissons that would support the trucks, tanks, and men unloaded from larger ships. Building a protected harbor in the rough seas would be a challenging task on its own—doing it under enemy fire in 18 days was unimaginable.

Superman was one of the many tugs struggling to position the Gooseberry ships and assemble the piers. German small arms fire and artillery zeroed in on the tugs and other Navy vessels as they operated near the shore and nightly air raids made the entire task both harrowing and exhausting.

A German counterattack was still entirely possible, yet news in the U.S. and Britain already celebrated success. According to these reports, a defeated German army was falling back from the surprise attack and victory was at hand. But their optimism was belied by artillery shells falling in the waters off Normandy and fierce resistance on land. Everyone involved in Task Force 128 knew the truth: if they were succeeding it was by the skin of their teeth. A massive influx of equipment and men was needed to sustain the foothold in France and precious little time remained before the Germans would push the entire operation back into the sea.

Now six days after the landing (D-Day +6), the floating roadways named Whales as well as the massive concrete caissons called Phoenix units were slated to arrive in the waters off France. But some of the Whales did not arrive. *Superman* was about to find out why.

What the crew of the *Superman* spotted on June 12 would have appeared odd to anyone unfamiliar with the plans to build an artificial harbor. It looked like a span of a suspension railroad bridge adrift at sea. In fact, it was Whale Tow 528, one of the floating spans of roadway for Operation Mulberry. But the ship responsible for delivering it, the USS *Partridge,* was nowhere to be seen.

Superman signaled the unit and, after no reply was received, approached cautiously. Closer to the structure was a grim hint of what had happened. An oil slick spread across the sea along with floating debris. Mooring alongside the unit, several of the crew boarded and found evidence of the *Partridge*'s fate. Clothing, lifejackets, shoes, and other personal effects were scattered about the bridge. A tent, used by a two-man anti-aircraft crew as shelter while crossing the English Channel, stood empty and stained with blood. Blood also covered the deck, mixing with the debris and salt spray. None of the crew was found.

It was clear that the *Partridge* was lost from a torpedo, a mine, or an air strike. But what happened to the men aboard? Had they been rescued? Captured? Or had they, too, vanished beneath the waves?

There wasn't time to speculate. The *Superman* rigged Whale Tow 528 and began to tow the bridge onto shore, leaving behind only a stain of oil on the surface of the Channel waters.

Two months earlier, in April 1944, two U.S. Navy officers boarded a train outside the dry docks in Tilbury, England, bound for London. They were a nondescript pair joining a sea of American soldiers and sailors that had flooded into Britain, mostly in the last year. They were from the U.S. Navy Minesweeper and Fleet Tug USS *Partridge.*

Although these were extraordinary times, this was an ordinary journey. Their trip to London was one traveled by many of those who went to receive carefully guarded orders from the admiralty headquarters to carry by hand back to their ships. However, Chief Boatswain Joe Cooney and Ensign Michael B. Rich were about to set into motion a series of events altering their own lives and careers, as well as those of their crew mates and the skipper of their ship.

When they walked through the door of the operation command office, they began a conversation highly unusual for the normally staid naval bureaucracy, an organization that strictly adheres, even today, to a chain of command for even the most minor interactions. The talk between two low-ranking reserve officers and a higher-ranking regular Navy officer was candid. Something was deeply wrong aboard their ship and they were getting a chance to do something neither one of them thought possible: air their concerns with the Navy brass above their captain.

The story they conveyed to the admiral would be echoed a decade later in Herman Wouk's *The Caine Mutiny.* The ships *Caine* and the *Partridge* sailed in parallel worlds and shared many traits. Both were minesweepers. Both were small, dilapidated ships built for another purpose in another war. Both had dedicated, skilled crews who were far removed from the formal, structured navies of battleships and aircraft carriers. Both had captains who exhibited paranoia; isolating themselves from officers, distrusting advice, and forcing their ships and crew to the brink of disaster at sea. Both had crews that fed their captain's paranoia, sending their

10

command into a downward spiral. Both were ships whose captains were removed from command in the middle of epic struggles of WWII. But the *Caine* existed solely in a work of fiction. The *Partridge* was real.

My grandfather served aboard the *Partridge* as a gunners mate. He would often talk about his time in the Navy as we floated homemade wooden boats down the Antietam Creek near my grandparents' home in Chewsville, Maryland. In between the stories about dodging German subs in the blue waters of the Caribbean and preparations for the D-Day invasion in the frigid English Channel, there were tales of a captain gone mad and uncanny similarities to a book called *The Caine Mutiny.*

As I grew up, the story calcified into family legend. The topic would come up every few years, usually when Humphrey Bogart appeared on television as Captain Queeg. And then it hardly came up at all. The war films of the 1950s seemed irrelevant and even trite to me and probably to a good deal of a generation growing up in the shadow of Vietnam. The 1954 film version of *Caine* features a scene where José Ferrer throws champagne in the face of Fred McMurray—a quaint set piece sharing more in common with white-gloved 18th-century duels than protracted guerrilla wars, terrorism, and the threat of nuclear war.

In the late 1990s I shared in the collective realization that my grandparents' generation had faced a wartime reality that was much harsher than Hollywood depicted with heroic speeches and marches into the sunset. They did not live in a simpler, less complex time; Hollywood only made it seem that way. Curiosity about my family's history led to a renewed interest in the *Caine* connection. I didn't expect to find much. Maybe only a brief mention in a Wikipedia article or an online forum. Instead, I found nothing.

Searches on the *Partridge* turned up little more than a paragraph on her general history and some mail bearing her postmark from the 1930s for sale on eBay. Searching for the true story of the *Caine Mutiny* turned up only ships that came after the book was published and the movie released: reflections of fiction in reality. Even if the *Partridge* was only a footnote in history as the true story of the *Caine Mutiny*, either that footnote was missing or it never had much truth in it.

Twenty years after my grandfather passed away, I put the questions to my dad. How similar were the stories? Was the drama of the *Partridge* really comparable to Wouk's story? How many details really match? Was it possible that it was all just a distortion through the lens of time? After all, it was long ago and maybe it was time to admit that an old family story was just that. Everyone in the Navy probably had a Captain Queeg in their war.

But his reply back to me was unwavering, expressing in no uncertain terms that it all had happened. It was all true. All the hallmarks of the book were there. Cut tow lines. Mocking songs. Even a missing quantity of canned fruit. He refreshed my memory with a laundry list of other similarities between the events of the *Caine* and what happened aboard the *Partridge*. And he had a list of living crew members. I commented that someone should talk to the men on that list and write about the ship and its connection to *Caine*.

"If someone is going to do that," he said. "They should do it fast."

Everyone on that list was over 80 years of age. There wouldn't be much time left to hear their stories.

There wasn't a choice. The *Partridge* wasn't just another war story; it was a hole in history. Whether or not I could prove that Herman Wouk was inspired by the *Partridge* was beside the point. A version of the story existed. It had happened before *The Caine Mutiny* was written. And I had a list of people who had lived every moment of it.

Wouk's novel ends with wistful melancholy as the *Caine* is scrapped after the war. Willie Keith, the central protagonist, looks back on his youthful folly that contributed to the mutiny and marvels at how the war has changed him. Many of the central players in the *Partridge*'s story were killed or severely injured shortly after their captain was relieved of command. Their story has never been told. Their perspectives have never been added to the discussion about the nature of command at sea.

If the *Caine*'s story were told in the pages of a novel, where would the *Partridge*'s story be told? If Wouk judged the officers and crew of the *Caine* harshly for their actions, what was the verdict on the *Partridge* and her crew? If Wouk had a voice in the matter, what about the voices of Joe Cooney, Mike Rich, Bill Ames, Tom Buffum, Frank Lefavor, and the rest of the officers and crew from the *Partridge*?

In researching this book, I set off to find out if the *Partridge* was truly the inspiration for *Caine*. Instead, I found another story, about people caught up in a narrative that would affect who they were in the war and what they would become afterward. This is the story of the USS *Partridge*, her crew and commanders, and the part she played in the war fought in the Atlantic and off the coast of Normandy. It's a story of violence, courage, camaraderie, and the topsy-turvy world of military justice.

It is a true, untold story from a time and place that has profoundly shaped how we measure heroism, sacrifice, and honor.

The struggle of her officers and crew to serve under an incompetent leader while skirting mutiny is what made the *Partridge* the template for the *Caine Mutiny*. It is a story that still resonates today, many years after the *Superman* left the oily spot in the ocean and the last traces of the little minesweeper dissipated beneath the waves.

Chapter 1
The Bird Boats

As peace fell across Europe in the winter of 1918, the continent was left with a long, gaping wound running in a jagged line from North to South. Fortified trenches zigzagged along a muddy, cratered landscape stitched together by miles and miles of barbed wire. Flying over Europe that year, a spectator would have seen a nearly unbroken wall from the Swiss frontier to the North Sea, across which two great armies had slaughtered each other with artillery, machine guns, gas, and bayonets in over four years of intense conflict.

This open wound of the Western Front existed in the landscape and within the minds and bodies of the people who fought along it. It was a wound that would never fully heal, evidenced today by the unexploded shells still cordoned off, buried deep underground waiting to either detonate or rust away for a hundred more years.

But if that air traveler were to disembark at the frigid waters of the North Sea and continue the journey underwater, he would come across a different kind of wall, just as menacing and deadly and, some would say, just as senseless. It was a fortification so lethal and complete that it would take a precious few additional lives after the Armistice from the roster of those sent to dismantle it.

This was The Northern Barrage: over 80,000 submerged mines stretching from the Orkney Islands in Scotland to the coast of Norway. This undersea wall, over 230 miles long, was created by the United States and Britain to pen in Germany's naval forces and reduce the U-boat menace—a weapon of war so effective that it had threatened to cut off Britain and France from the rest of the world.

Laying down such a vast quantity of mines was a daunting and dangerous task—so much so that little thought was given to how they would be cleaned up. Britain was initially against the idea of creating the undersea wall of mines, but the U.S. Navy pressed ahead, finishing just as the war ended. The Northern Barrage was like many strategies of WWI: massive, fixed, and accomplishing little to bring about a decisive victory. After the war ended, the U.S. Navy had to pay for its ambition by dismantling the deadly barrier.

The ingenuity applied to marine mining at the time spoke to an age of mechanized war in a dangerous adolescence. Modern weapons could hurl artillery miles over the horizon, wipe out a platoon of men with a spray of bullets, and kill or maim scores more with inescapable poison gas. And yet this technology did little more than pin each side down, sapping the will of nations to supply fresh bodies to the cause. It was an age of indiscriminate, but absolute, destruction.

The formidable undersea barrier would, until it was removed, cut off desperately needed postwar maritime traffic. Exacerbating the problem was the use of novel technology devised to make mines more difficult to evade and sweep. The mines in the Northern Barrage sat below the surface of the water and were magnetically activated. They were innovative devices with one crucial flaw: there were no existing methods for their removal.

As the war wound down, it was clear that this wall of mines would become a peacetime liability—an obstacle to the free trade the Allies had fought so hard to achieve. The U.S. Navy began work on a class of minesweeper up to the task of clearing one of the largest undersea barriers ever created. But with wartime budgets drastically cut, it needed to build vessels that could be used for a wide range of tasks.

The Navy's answer was the Lapwing Minesweeper. These small, steel-hulled ships were tough, versatile, and equipped with a degaussing circuit to make them invisible to the magnetic mines they passed over. Built in shipyards from Alabama to New York City, the Lapwing class minesweepers were still under construction as the war ended.

With names like *Osprey, Robin, Flamingo, Partridge,* and *Owl,* the 49 ships, dubbed Bird Boats, were less than a formidable force. Measuring 187 feet, 10 inches in length and made for a crew of about 60 with minimal armament, the ships made up for their small size with power and versatility. A single-screw 1,400 horsepower reciprocating steam engine, heavy winches, and an aft boom made them ideal for towing and construction support. The engine employed increasing piston sizes as the expanding steam passed through the engine. The result was tremendous torque at relatively low revolutions, greatly increasing their towing capacity. This was a capability that proved valuable in the Northern Barrage operation and later during WWII.

Oddly, the ships were equipped with sails. The feature was probably added to retain some mobility in a minefield if the engines were disabled by an explosion, but their presence was an immediate mystery and remained a source of amusement throughout the *Lapwing's* service. A convoy of the little boats steaming for Europe in 1919 managed to get about two knots additional speed with the sail up and their engines pumping. Other ad hoc uses were found throughout the years. In 1925, while serving as a seaplane tender, the *Pelican* managed to get to port after engine failure by removing canvass from its attached aircraft and using it in place of its missing sailcloth. Bill Ames, who served aboard the *Partridge* from 1941 to 1944 as a Signalman, Chief Master at Arms, and Chief Quartermaster, recalled that the crew tested this antiquated feature in the Caribbean out of curiosity and managed to move the ship slowly through the water.

Clearing the Northern Barrage was one of the most hazardous duties of the U.S. Navy between the wars. The 230-mile minefield was formidable, as wide as 3,500 feet in some places. The mines had long antennae extending from the main body moored to the ocean floor. These sensitive antennae expanded the range of the mines, causing them to explode at the detection of even a small amount of metal passing nearby. A chain reaction often ensued, turning large areas of the water into a boiling sea. If mine warfare wasn't precise, it was at least thorough.

In the winter of 1918, two wooden fishing vessels, the *Red Fern* and *Red Rose,* were towed to the barrage from a base in Scotland. The two small ships then set off into the minefield with a sweep line strung between them. This mission was a test run meant to determine if the mines were still active, but the Navy had considered using these small wooden fishing vessels for the entire mission. The near-disaster that followed confirmed the decision to build the tough Bird Boats to clear the entire minefield instead.

The *Fern* and the *Rose* were prepared to evade the mines' magnetic detectors by sinking all nail holes, covering all metal parts, caulking seams, and applying a heavy coat of tar to their hulls. A serrated rope was strung between the two ships to cut the mine mooring lines and bring them safely to the surface. That was, at least, the theory.

On December 22, 1918, the ships sailed into the barrage and the effectiveness of the minefield immediately became apparent. Minutes after their mission began, a huge column of discolored water burst into the air close to the *Rose*. The force of the explosion nearly destroyed the hull of the ship and she quickly began to take on water. The crew started pumps but they just barely kept up with the water seeping in through the damaged hull. Still, the official report on the sweeping operation is upbeat in its assessment of the ships, which continued operation despite the damage:

> *"It was a pretty sight to see these little craft sailing* back *and forth across the mine field, wearing and tacking in unison, and keeping station on each other by furling topsails or streaming sea anchors."*

The little boats confirmed their test several times over the next three hours, exploding six more mines, and further damaging their hulls. But another hazard of the operation quickly became apparent: the weather. By three o'clock the sun had already set on the Northern hemisphere, cutting off the *Rose* and *Fern* from their towing vessels, the *Patapsco* and *Patuxent*. The barometer began to drop rapidly and a storm with hurricane-force winds descended on the ships.

The storm raged for three days and, although the *Patapsco* and *Patuxent* returned to their base, the *Rose* and *Fern* were presumed lost amid the raging storm and exploding mines. Miraculously, however, the two ships survived. On Christmas Eve, the *Rose*, badly damaged, managed to reach Peterhead, Scotland. The next day, the *Fern* anchored at St. Andrews Bay, some 200 miles from her intended destination.

These first tests in modern minesweeping proved that the Bird Boats, now on their way across the Atlantic, would face daunting perils of weather, new technology, and high explosives in their mission.

The first of the Lapwing sweepers arrived in summer, giving them more daylight hours in the water and safer weather conditions. Their operation was covered by Yeoman First Class Elmer M. Ziegler writing for the Navy publication *The Recruit*. Ziegler described how the sweeping was actually accomplished:

> *"The sweeping is done by pairs of the larger vessels such as the Eider, Teal, Turkey, Swallow, etc., steaming across the mine field separated from each other by about 600 yards and towing a heavy serrated wire rope between them, the height of which is kept sixty fathoms below the surface by means of two metal kites. Each pair of sweeper is followed by a sub chaser armed with rifles and machine guns with which the mines are peppered as they pop up to the surface of the water."*

Ziegler also marveled at the modernity of the Sweeper Fleet, particularly its communication system:

> *The wireless telephone, with which all the sweepers and chasers are equipped, is the most used instrument at sea. It is no more uncommon for an officer to be called from his dinner by a messenger boy announcing that he is "wanted on the 'phone'" than for a businessman or doctor in civilian life.*

But this was no place for businessmen casually taking phone calls. The sweeping operation proved dangerous and deadly. Before she even began to sweep, the *Auk* lost a Boatswain's Mate, who was crushed between the wrist pin bearing of the engine and the sweeping drum. During the sweep on July 9, a heavy storm sparked a chain reaction near the *Auk* and *Patuxent,* causing a sweep kite to be lost and 70 meters of sweep wire to be carried away.

Later in the day, the *Pelican* set off a series of five mines under similar conditions, badly damaging the ship. With the *Auk* and *Eider* on either side, the *Pelican* was able to stay afloat and be assisted toward Scotland. Even with pumps working, the forward compartments of the ship were completely flooded. Water pressure built up and the hull began to buckle. Most of her crew were transferred to the sister vessels in tow, but her captain, Lt. Bulmer, stayed aboard and is credited with getting the ship to shore (tragically, Bulmer died a few weeks later in a car accident).

The *Bobolink* had a face-to-face encounter with a mine when pulling in her sweep. The explosive object lodged itself into the kite wire and was hoisted aboard

21

the ship. When the ship's commander, Lieutenant Frank Bruce, attempted to clear the mine, it unexpectedly exploded, killing him instantly. Four other crew members were thrown overboard and the ship was seriously damaged, the hull plating driven in as much as two to three feet in some places. Her rudder was gone, the propeller twisted beyond repair, and the engine thrown out of line. The boat seemed to be a total loss, but, with the assistance of the *Teal* and *Swallow*, she made it to shore through a dense fog.

As the sweep operation continued, exploding mines continued to inflict tolls on the ships and sailors as they slowly moved across the long stretch of sea. These dangers, largely unrecognized back home, were reflected somewhat bitterly in a poem quoted by Ziegler (he attributes it only to "a yeoman who is 'over there' now").

> *The mothers of soldiers are smiling—*
> *Their boys are returning home,*
> *But some still weep for their boys on the deep*
> *In the midst of that mine-filled zone.*
> *There is never an enemy present—*
> *We're undoing the work we have done,*
> *Yet do not forget the danger we face—*
> *They are as great as when war was begun*
> *Our work is raising the bombs*
> *We set to entrap our dread foe,*
> *And the dangers that lurk with this kind of work*
> *Only those who have faced them can know.*

Sailors did face great danger. Many were injured or lost their lives working with the dangerous and erratic serrated wire strung between two vessels and the unpredictable mines. Notably, however, none of the Lapwing ships were lost. It seems that what the ships lacked in preventing underwater explosions, they more than made up for in an ability to stay afloat and tow each other to safety.

Time and again, badly damaged ships would be helped by other Lapwings just barely making it to port for repairs. The ships surprised many with their ability to withstand the notoriously rough North Sea. This combination of resilience and towing power was an important asset during one of the last deadly operations of World War I.

From an age where military specialization is highly valued, it is difficult to understand a Navy that was frugal with its resources. The Lapwings were built as minesweepers but were designed to handle an array of towing, salvage, and rescue operations. These characteristics made the ships an excellent investment that would pay off with extensive and varied service between the wars and through WWII. The Northern Barrage is where the story of the *Partridge* begins. The ship was built for one mission, but had the capacity to be used for just about anything thrown at her. In the coming decades, just about everything was.

If World War I was defined by broad, sometimes rash tactics that led to a stalemate, the strategists of World War II specifically looked to avoid stalemate. The Germans used quick mechanized lightning attacks called Blitzkrieg to punch holes in enemy lines to great effect at the beginning of the war. To counter, the Allies planned an amphibious assault on Normandy. And they would support it with an innovation of their own. They would build an artificial harbor that would ensure that the Allies could move ashore quickly through the element of surprise—the Germans simply could not believe the invasion would take place where no major harbor existed. At the same time, Allied armies would receive a steady supply of food, fuel, equipment, and ammunition.

The *Partridge* and many of her sister ships were called on to perform one of the most audacious projects of the war in support of the D-Day invasion. The capability of these ships to serve as tug boats and also survive the unpredictable weather in the English Channel was sorely needed in an operation known as Mulberry.

Prior to taking part in this massive armada, however, the Lapwing ships endured the chaos the U.S. Navy struggled through in the early days of the war. As the front line against attacks by the Japanese Navy in the Pacific and German subs in the Atlantic, the Navy was ill prepared. The country had a significantly smaller navy than the Axis powers, with outdated ships and equipment—weaknesses that Germany and Japan were counting on to win a swift negotiated peace. With shipping cut off from both the Atlantic and Pacific, a weak Navy meant that the U.S. industrial machine could not gear up for war and could do little more than defend America's shores.

As America's Pacific fleet struggled to rebuild itself after the attack on Pearl Harbor, the U.S. fought to keep shipping lanes open in the Atlantic seaboard. From the Lapwings' impressive performance at Pearl Harbor (the *Auk* successfully defended herself against four waves of attacks by Japanese bombers, eventually bringing down two planes) to their salvage and towing operations in the Caribbean and the Gulf of Mexico, the Navy depended on these craft, which were older than the majority of their crews.

But back in 1919, war seemed to be in the past for the Bird Boats. After clearing the Northern Barrage, the little boats set sail for a tour of Europe, entering ports along the coast of France and Portugal and throughout the Mediterranean and finally heading for home. The Lapwings were reviewed in New York on November 24, 1919, by the Secretary of the Navy, Josephus Daniels. Officers and their wives attended a reception held by the Secretary aboard the USS *Columbia* while the crew of over 2,000 attended a luncheon hosted by the Knights of Columbus at the Astor Hotel in Manhattan. The Navy congratulated itself on ridding the world of a menace of its own creation. In *The Northern Barrage,* published in 1920 under the direction of Daniels, taking up the mines is celebrated as a triumph even over its own folly:

"In five months the building of a barrier of mines from Scotland to Norway had been accomplished. Peace came and in less than 11 months after the signing of the armistice the task of removing those same mines had been completed; and insofar as mines laid by the United States Navy were concerned as a menace to navigation the North Sea was again made safe for world commerce."

While the mines may have been taken up efficiently, it's debatable whether the Northern Barrage was worth the money, equipment, and lives it took to remove it. The massive project sank only two German U-boats. And, although it was officially said to have stopped 30 percent of U-boat traffic, some put this figure at closer to 10 percent.

At midnight on November 24, 1919, the flag was lowered on the North Sea Mine Force, ending the mission the Lapwings had been built for. While older submarine chasers were decommissioned after the mission and sold, the Navy brass was busy trying to figure out what to do with the new Bird Boats. There seemed to be no conclusive answer. In the decades to follow, Bird Boats saw duty dredging harbors, tending seaplanes, participating in scientific surveys, observing eclipses, escorting convoys, towing targets, and other odd jobs the Navy needed to get done. These were the duties under which the *Partridge* aged gracefully for the next 20 years.

Two men who would serve aboard the *Partridge* during World War II also saw service during the Great War: Adnah Caldin, a non-commissioned career officer who saw the *Partridge's* command as an opportunity, at last, to advance within the Navy he had dutifully served for two decades; and Joe Cooney, the citizen sailor who left the Navy after his service in WWI to work the busy waterways of New York Harbor, only to return as a reservist in his middle age. In both their leadership style and personal history, these two men are examples of the polar forces that would impact the *Partridge* during WWII. They were the long-serving career Navy and the working man's Navy, the spit-and-polish discipline and the grimy work-a-day reality. And, in some ways, both were, like the *Partridge*, cast aside or neglected until an hour of need.

The roots of the *Partridge* story lie in her beginnings as part of a forgotten campaign to rid the world of a menace the U.S. Navy itself created. It was the kind of work that didn't advance the careers of her commanding officers, didn't make headlines, and required methodic, tedious seamanship. For many of her commanding officers, these experiences were a fine heritage that suited them and their crews. But for one commander, Lt. Adnah Caldin, the hodgepodge, workaday nature of the ship conspired against even his best intentions.

Chapter 2
Lieutenant Wouk's Memo

The sound of keystrokes from the Underwood manual typewriter echoed throughout the DMS *Southard* and spilled into the tropical South Pacific night. It was a common sound aboard any U.S. Navy vessel during WWII. Ships' logs, war diaries, battle reports—the minutia of life at sea was recorded across the ribbons of tens of thousands of typewriters, often by men struggling to hunt-and-peck out just a few lines. So many typewriters were needed by the military during the war that it was actually illegal for a civilian to purchase one.

But the Navy officer who worked the keys on this night in August 1945, during the waning days of the Pacific war, was writing something in a wholly different rhythm from the staccato, toneless voice of so many Navy documents. Tonight, he was letting his passion for writing take over, spilling out page after page on the nature of command at sea, civilians serving their country in a time of war, and needed reforms in leadership structure—particularly that of ships' captains. It was an audacious proposal, particularly coming from a U.S. Navy Reserve lieutenant who had served less than four years. It was addressed to the Secretary of the Navy.

The men aboard the small ship had grown accustomed to the sound of tapping echoing throughout the ancient minesweeper. If their peculiar Executive Officer wasn't typing lengthy memos to the highest echelons of Navy command, he was working on his novel. Some said he was a famous author; some said he was a gag writer in Hollywood. Others said he was just another "90-day wonder" (an officer rushed through 90 days of training) who would sink back into anonymity once this war was over—after all, everybody claimed to know somebody who was a novelist or a movie star back home and a few even claimed to be one.

The tapping of the keys came to a sudden stop as the General Quarters whistle sounded throughout the ship. Leaving the half-finished memo, the lieutenant raced to the bridge. At this late stage in the war, Japanese planes were plunging out of the sky, and no ship in the U.S. Pacific Fleet was immune to this deadly new turn in the war. Writing about the nature of command at sea would, for now, have to wait. There was a war to fight and Lt. Herman Wouk was needed on the bridge.

For the men and women serving in the Allied fleets of the Pacific in 1945, victory was close at hand, but bore a heavy price. The Japanese had proven to be ruthless defenders, bitterly fighting to the death in hundreds of island campaigns, and they were only hardening their resolve as defeat became imminent. Kamikaze attacks on U.S. warships increased in frequency, a sign of the price many Japanese were willing to pay to defend their homeland from invasion. Airplanes by the hundreds screamed down from the sky on the American fleets invading Okinawa and Iwo Jima. As victory came in

Europe, it was clear to the soldiers and sailors preparing for the final push that the worst was still ahead.

The word Kamikaze refers to another challenge that soldiers and sailors faced as they fought the final stages of the war: the weather. It is most often translated into English as "Divine Wind," but Kamikaze refers specifically to a combination of storms that knocked out two Mongolian fleets under the command of Kublai Khan in 1274 and 1281. Now in 1945, Americans fighting in the Pacific faced the same threat that gave the suicide planes their namesake: typhoons.

Typhoons and hurricanes are essentially the same kind of storm; only the names in the Pacific and Atlantic are changed. There is one important difference: typhoons can occur throughout the year and in greater frequency. But their occurrence can be unpredictable. In 1943, for example, no storms were reported at all. But in 1944-45, typhoons wrought havoc on the massive American build-up to the invasion of Japan. While the typhoons did not ultimately change the course of the war, they made its conclusion that much more uncertain and difficult.

On December 17, 1944, Typhoon *Cobra* or *Halsey's Typhoon* hit Task Force 38 returning from supporting the invasion of the Philippines. Three destroyers were lost and 790 sailors killed. One-hundred and forty-six aircraft were lost or damaged beyond repair and a cruiser, five aircraft carriers, and three destroyers suffered serious damage. By comparison, the Battle of Midway cost the Americans 307 lives, 98 aircraft, one carrier, and one destroyer.

Typhoon *Ursula* in September 1945 brought down over 30 U.S. aircraft transporting POWs to the Philippines. This disaster, still considered the worst in aviation history, claimed the lives of over 900 serviceman.

Later that month, Typhoon *Ida* passed through Okinawa with minor damage to U.S. forces but hit the Japanese mainland, killing more than 3,500 people onshore and at sea. Typhoon *Louise* in October 1945 took fewer lives (36 soldiers and sailors lost on or near Okinawa), but the destruction of equipment was massive. Food stores were down to as little as 10 days' worth and medical supplies and equipment were scarce; 12 ships were sunk, 222 ships grounded, and another 32 heavily damaged. Had Japan not surrendered in August 1945 as a result of the atomic attacks on Nagasaki and Hiroshima, the invasion surely would have been delayed due to the destruction to equipment and supplies.

The decision to use atomic weapons against Japan rested with high-level civilian and military officials—and even they were uncertain of the outcome the blasts would produce. As far as the average soldier, sailor, and marine knew before news of the surrender reached them, the war would continue for years. And even after the bombs were dropped and Japan did surrender, home for most soldiers and sailors was still very far away. The typhoons that struck in 1945 made the end of the long, bloody conflict that much more arduous and difficult to bear.

Lt. Herman Wouk was one of the many Navy reservists stuck in limbo between the end of the war and home. He had served for over four years, rising in rank from ensign to lieutenant. He was slated to take command of the DMS *Southard*, a converted destroyer minesweeper built in 1919 on which he had served as Executive Officer since 1944. Commanding the ship on her way home was to be his final duty at sea. But for now, the DMS *Southard* was not going anywhere. Passage home was blocked by relentless typhoons and coral reefs.

In October 1945—two months after the Japanese surrender—the *Southard* sat stranded on a reef off of Tsuken Shima, a small island near Buckner Bay in Okinawa. She was thrown onto the reef by a combination of winds blowing up to 140 miles per hour and waves that reached 36 feet.

This wasn't the *Southard's* first encounter with a typhoon. Just a month earlier, she had been hit by Typhoon *Ida*. Although the ship weathered the storm, a submarine net tangled in her propeller. With no power, she was helpless against the storm and grounded on a pinnacle reef. Divers and repair crews were able to re-float the ship and get her running, at least to make it back to the U.S. to salvage for scrap. But even this final mission was not meant to be.

It was the notorious Typhoon *Louise* that would finally do in the *Southard*, robbing the ship of a final duty to her country: transporting her crew home. Now the *Southard* sat still in the water. Wouk took command of the ship when the captain left with most of the crew. Now he commanded a grounded ship and a skeleton crew of fewer than a dozen sailors to do whatever could be done to keep the ship afloat, or at least take charge of her if she broke free.

Wouk was typical of many of the officers who entered the Navy at the beginning of the war as ensigns and rose through the ranks, often ending the war with their own command. Only two months before, the lieutenant's unplanned naval career seemed to stretch before him. As far as he knew, after he took command of the *Southard*, he might remain her skipper for many years to come. Although the Navy had never been in the young officer's plans, he had settled into life at sea and had begun to view the Navy as his own, just as much as the career officers that served alongside and above him; his admiration for the Navy would stay with him for the rest of his life.

But now, instead of commanding a vessel at sea, Wouk was left in charge of a motionless wreck in a remote part of the world with a tiny crew all contemplating, along with him, the quickest trip back home. The lieutenant had spent his idle time at sea writing a novel and had sold it to a publisher back home. In the end, he would return to civilian life and begin life as a writer—something he had dreamed of for years. The Navy had given him adventure and experience; now getting home and getting out was his priority.

But a quick route home was not in the cards. The ship's familiar bob was replaced by an eerie calm; the sounds of men moving about the ship were reduced to a minimum. The precautions to black out her lights were now useless. All was still in the hot night air.

With nowhere to go, no war to fight, and no crew to manage, the executive officer had little to do but enter into a log book, night after night, words less auspicious than the ones he addressed to the Secretary of the Navy just two months ago when the war was raging and the Navy was still his life. This was no memo to change the Navy and it certainly wasn't a novel. These were simple, dull entries made night after night:

Aground as before.
Lieutenant Herman Wouk, USNR

Herman Wouk's literary career is most prominently linked to the events of World War II. Although he has written dozens of novels and works of nonfiction on topics ranging from Judaism to life in the Caribbean, he is most famous for his World War II novels, *The Caine Mutiny*, *The Winds of War*, and *War and Remembrance*. *Caine* is his most personal war novel, drawing directly on his experiences serving aboard two destroyer minesweepers in the Pacific.

Wouk grew up in New York City, the son of Jewish Russian immigrants. The family initially settled in an Orthodox community in the Bronx. His father's laundry business became increasingly successful and the family eventually moved to Manhattan. Wouk knew from an early age that he wanted to be a writer, but his family encouraged it only as a hobby; they believed that law would be a better choice for him, since he had done well in school and was accepted at Columbia University.

Wouk disappointed his parents by announcing writing as a career choice during his early college days. Unlike many writers, however, he found success fairly quickly. Soon after graduation, he landed jobs writing jokes for Borscht Belt comedians and was eventually hired by the radio star Fred Allen to write gags, pulling in a substantial salary uncommon in the 1930s. After his initial success, Wouk expressed interest in serving his country as war loomed on the horizon and he entered into service as a "dollar-a-year man," writing radio plays for the U.S. treasury department. (Dollar-a-year men were professionals who essentially donated their services to government agencies for the nominal salary of a dollar a year.)

Wouk had tried to enter the Navy's officer training program in the early 1940s but an engineering requirement kept him out. After Pearl Harbor, the Navy became less selective and he was taken in as an officer candidate attending Midshipman's School at Columbia. After graduating in the top 20 of his class, he was assigned to the Pacific aboard the *Zane*, a WWI four-stack destroyer minesweeper. Like all minesweepers of the era, the *Zane* spent little time sweeping mines, instead performing patrolling and screening duties as well as target and other auxiliary towing. Wouk saw action as part of Operation Flintlock, the invasion of the Marshall Islands, and Operation Forager, the invasion of the Marianas islands. His ship won six battle stars for action throughout the Pacific.

The *Southard*, on which Wouk served from 1944 until the end of the war, was a Clemson class four-stack destroyer that had received 10 battle stars in the war, despite her 26 years of age. She screened convoys in the South Pacific between Espiritu Santo, Efate, Nouméa, Tulagi, Purvis Bay, and Guadalcanal. The ship sunk a sub off Guadalcanal, took part in the bombardment of Bougainville, swept mines in the Leyte Gulf, and survived two kamikaze attacks—one just missed the ship and the other left the plane's engine embedded in the ship's aft. Wouk was aboard when the second kamikaze attacked and saw the horrific damage it inflicted—a memory he would record in a similar incident in *The Caine Mutiny*.

Caine follows the naval career of Willie Keith, a kid from a privileged background who joins the Navy and is trained as an officer. He is assigned to the USS *Caine*. The ship is competently run by her commanding officer,

DeVries, who, while unconventional, is able to bring out the best in his reserve officers—men like Steve Maryk, a fisherman who dreams of joining the "real" Navy out of the reserves, and aspiring author Tom Keefer who works on his novel during his off hours but serves as an able, if acerbic, communications officer. But the idealistic Keith is relieved when the less-than-by-the-book Captain DeVries is transferred to another ship and replaced by the more disciplined Phillip Francis Queeg.

Queeg, however, quickly alienates himself from his officers and crew by doling out harsh punishments and placing a higher value on personal appearance than performance.

For example, while chewing out a crew member for having loose shirt tails, he neglects the course of his ship, runs a full circle, and cuts the ship's own tow line. During the invasion of Kwajalein, Queeg panics under fire and orders the *Caine* to abandon its escort of a landing craft too far from the shore, dumping a yellow marker instead to indicate its correct course. This earns him the unaffectionate nickname "Old Yellow Stain" from the crew. Finally, and most famously, he orders the ship turned upside down to find a duplicate key to the store room because one cup of strawberries is missing.

The intellectual Tom Keefer convinces Executive Officer Steve Maryk that Queeg exhibits symptoms of a paranoid schizophrenic and encourages him to begin a log recording the captain's behavior. When the two have a chance to meet with Admiral Halsey about the matter, however, Keefer loses his nerve and convinces Maryk that their pleas will fall on deaf ears and could be harmful to their careers.

Later, during a typhoon, Queeg and Maryk clash over the best way to weather the storm. Maryk takes over command from Queeg and is supported by Willie Keith. The ship is saved but Maryk and Keith are accused of mutiny. A trial ensues, with Maryk defended reluctantly by a brilliant attorney-turned-Navy-pilot Barney Greenwald. Keefer denies any involvement, thus weakening Maryk's case, but Greenwald forces Queeg into a breakdown while on the stand in what has become one of the most iconic images in cinema and literary history. After forcing Queeg to face his many failings in command, Greenwald essentially lets the Captain of the *Caine* hang himself in a rant about missing strawberries and a search for a stolen key, all while he nervously fiddles with a pair of ball bearings in his hand:

> *"He hardly paused for breath. He seemed unable to pause. His narrative became less distinct as he talked, his jumps in time and place more sudden and harder to follow. He talked on and on, rolling the balls, his face glowing with satisfaction as he scored all these successive points in his vindication."*

It's a stunning scene in the novel and on film. When Humphrey Bogart completed it, the cast and crew on the set burst into applause. It's a moment of powerful self-destruction that affirms the actions of Maryk and Keith and, ultimately, condemns Queeg.

Maryk is acquitted and the case against Keith is never pursued. But, although he is the one to exploit Queeg's weaknesses on the stand, Greenwald drunkenly dresses down the *Caine's* officers, particularly Keefer, for their failure to support their captain.

"See, while I was studying law 'n' old Keefer here was writing his play for the Theatre Guild, and Willie here was on the playing fields of Prinshton, all that time these birds we call regulars—these stuffy, stupid Prussians, in the Navy and the Army were manning guns...Of course, we figured in those days, only fools go into armed service, bad pay, no millionaire future, and you can't call your mind or body your own. Not for sensitive intellectuals..."

"Yes, even Queeg, poor sad guy, yes, and most of them not sad at all, fellows, a lot of them sharper boys than any of us, don't kid yourself, best men I've ever seen, you can't be good in the Army or Navy unless you're goddamn good..."

Wouk took the "through-the-looking-glass" experience of a civilian thrust into military life from his own experience. His ascent from ensign to the second in command of the *Southard* in just three years parallels Ensign Keith's career as he moves from a know-it-all civilian to a naval officer with a deep respect for the military and its time-honored traditions.

The passages in *Caine* that touch on the violence and horror of war are few and far between, but still have great impact. After the trial, Keith experiences the horrors of a Kamikaze attack firsthand:

"The plane hit with the sound of cars colliding on a highway, and a second later there was an explosion. Willie's teeth grated as though he had been punched in the face, and his ears rang. He staggered erect. He could see a puff of blue-gray

smoke *curling up from behind the galley deckhouse, where the gun crew still sprawled in individual gray lumps."*

Later Keith sees the body of a dead sailor and the Kamikaze pilot:

"The water washed away for a few seconds, and the lantern beam showed the sailor clearly, pinned down and crushed by the battered engine of the Jap plane, his face and his dungarees black with grease. The sight reminded Willie of the mashed squirrels he had often seen lying on the roads of Manhasset on autumn mornings. It was shocking to soak in, all in an instant, the fact that people were as soft and destructible as squirrels."

"The remains of the Kamikaze pilot were frightful. Willie turned away after a glimpse of bones and charred purple meat, sitting position in the telescoped cockpit as though the dread thing were still flying; a double row of grinning yellow teeth burned all bare; and most appalling of all, undamaged goggles above the teeth sunk into the ruined face, giving it a live, peering look. The smell was like a butcher shop."

Wouk poured the nuts and bolts of life aboard the *Zane* and *Southard* into *The Caine Mutiny*. All three ships were destroyer minesweepers, stationed in the Pacific and well past their prime. The *Caine* participates in many of the battles and theaters of war that Wouk experienced firsthand.

But the book also reflects Wouk's perspective on the war as a reserve officer serving on a working ship, with the major conflict often just over the horizon, and as a civilian entering the sometimes difficult hierarchy of the U.S. Navy. The passages about the Kamikaze attack are dramatic, but they make up a small fraction of the book's main emphasis on routine, dull exercises and maneuvers, fatigue from watch duties, and tension and strife brought on by naval bureaucracy.

This book, about the duller side of war, was a surprise sensation. When it hit bookshelves in 1951, it became a commercial success. *Caine* earned the Pulitzer Prize for fiction in 1952 and replaced *From Here to Eternity* as the *New York Times* #1 Bestseller—a position it held for two and a half years. In 1954, Wouk's adaptation of the courtroom sequence from the novel, *The Caine Mutiny Court Martial*, opened on Broadway directed by Charles Laughton. Five months later, a film adaptation starring Humphrey Bogart was released. Bogart's depiction of Queeg, his last role on film, is widely regarded as one of his finest and has contributed to Queeg's ascension into a literary icon akin to Ahab, Bligh, and The Ancient Mariner—characters so ubiquitous that they are quoted and understood by people who have never read the original literature and history.

The story remains compelling to audiences today. *The Caine Mutiny Court Martial* continues to be produced on Broadway and the film is often cited as a classic. The novel is even taught in officers' training at Annapolis and, in all likelihood, will endure as one of the defining works of World War II. Part of the reason for the story's endurance is its unique perspective. While most WWII films and novels focus on the heroics and hellfire of battle, Wouk turns his attention to the mundane aspects of war. As a civilian entering Navy life, Willy Keith finds most of his time spent typing memos, decoding, and navigating the labyrinth of Navy bureaucracy and protocol rather than fighting the Japanese.

Despite its success and longevity, however, *Caine* has never been accepted into the literary canon. Some critics have lambasted Wouk's dimestore storytelling and the book's ending is contradictory and problematic. Greenwald's conclusion, and Wouk's, throws off most readers, perhaps because it is a certain, almost didactic lesson tacked on to a deeply ambiguous story. Were the officers of the *Caine* really supposed to follow Captain Queeg to their doom just because he had chosen the military as a career and they had not? Should they really have believed that no naval officer in command of a ship could possibly be incompetent and even insane?

If Wouk's military life is reflected in the ship's history, the theater of war, and even in specific battles, did he also know a real Queeg?

Wouk shares Keith's vantage point of his commanding officers. Both enter the Navy as educated young men from privileged backgrounds. In *Caine*, Willie Keith chafes under the command of the unorthodox, sloppy Captain Devries, his first commander, and the harsh, capricious Captain Queeg. But when asked about this, Wouk has said that his two actual commanding officers were exemplary in their performance and leadership.

In other words, Wouk did not base Queeg, arguably one of the most recognizable characters in the literature of our time, on anyone, least of all his commanding officers. He invented him. There was no real mutiny. There was no trial. In short, there was never a real Captain Queeg.

Wouk may not have served under any Queegs, but questions of command structure and how the absolute power of a captain at sea can exist in an otherwise libertine democracy were clearly important to the young reserve officer. It brings us back to that hot August night in 1945 with a war still raging. Prior to *Caine*, long before he was a famous author, Lieutenant Wouk typed a memo about the Navy and its professional officers and addressed it to the Secretary of the Navy. In the 25-page document, Wouk covered the topic of ship command structure throughout the fleet and said dramatic changes were desperately needed.

The memo is fueled by the passions of a young man who ardently believed that an age-old system needed to be reformed. With lips loosened by alcohol and tropical nights, officers told stories about commanders who were over-zealous, sticklers for regulation, or just plain vindictive. Some may have complained that it was the stupid and uncreative who were rewarded in the Navy and that a return to civilian life would show who was truly on top. Aboard the *Southard*, these stories swirled in Lieutenant Wouk's head as he hammered out his thoughts about the state of naval leadership, the morale of its men, and the waste of civilian talent he saw. In the 25 pages, he outlined what he perceived to be the problems with naval command.

"No topic is more popular in officers' clubs through the wide Pacific than 'Captain Bligh' stories of this war..."

And, no doubt, Bligh was cited by many a disgruntled crewman and officers serving under a tough, unyielding commander. Charles Laughton's portrayal of Bligh as a cruel madman in the film *Mutiny on the Bounty* (the Academy Award winner for Best Picture in 1936) certainly influenced men of the Navy more than the historical Bligh, and were probably Wouk's intended reference in the memo.

The young lieutenant, however, was not just complaining. He was outlining a path to reform. He went on to make recommendations for a new way the Navy could manage this problem—a recommendation that sounds more like an order to the Secretary of the Navy than a suggestion from a reserve officer.

Periodic reports shall be made by the officers of a vessel on the quality of the commanding officer...These reports shall not be seen by the commanding officer unless the Navy Dept. desires to bring them to his attention.

Wouk was writing not as an inexperienced Willy Keith, just coming aboard full of civvy optimism and reform. He had served for nearly four years in the Navy. After strict, if not extensive, officer's training and life aboard two Navy vessels, Wouk still saw the value of civilian protocols in the chain of command.

Justifiably or not, young men with a democratic upbringing feel deprived of human dignity and self-

44

respect in our wardrooms today, and military indoctrination does not change that sentiment.

It's as if Willy Keith were writing the memo in a world where there had been no grand conflict, no mutiny, no trial, and no dressing down from Greenwald. Here, Wouk is not a staunch supporter of Navy tradition; he is its reformer.

It's not likely that Wouk received a reply from the Secretary of the Navy. The sudden outbreak of peace had sent the wartime bureaucracy into chaos. With Kamikazes, mined waters, amphibious assaults, and submarine attacks behind him, Wouk eventually settled on the most familiar wartime feeling: boredom. Reform within the Navy had lost its interest for him. It was time to go home.

Stranded on a shallow reef in a remote part of the world, Wouk spent hot, tropical nights sweating over the Woodstock, pounding little more than letters home and the ship's log, night after night.

Aground as before...
Aground as before...

Pulling the paper from the typewriter every night, Wouk may have realized that his personal attempt at naval reform was altered by events much larger than himself or his ship: the end of the war. What a reservist felt about naval command was a moot point now. They were going home. Checking in on the skeleton crew one last time, Lieutenant Wouk turned in for the night, hoping tomorrow might bring an end to this boredom.

Maybe it was at this point, stranded on the reef, commanding a ship to nowhere, that he began to have doubts about what he had expressed in his memo. He didn't really believe men should hold power over their captain. All of the drunken proclamations from officers about the Ahabs and Blighs they served under were from reserve officers like him. Men whose devotion to the Navy lasted three or four years at best.

What about the men who had served their country for a decade or more before the war began and would continue well after the ticker-tape parades ended and most reservists went back to better-paying professional careers, where they could be near their family and friends? Be with their wives every night? See their children grow up?

Such men may have been harsh on their crews and not as quick to change routine for some wide-eyed reservists, but didn't they deserve support, respect, and admiration?

If Wouk didn't have these thoughts while stranded on the reef, he did feel it at some point in the years after the war. In fact, he would write a novel that could have been a response to his own memo. *Caine*'s 500-plus pages can be seen as a sharp rebuttal to a young reserve lieutenant's recommendations: It wasn't the Navy that could learn a thing or two from civilians, it was the other way around.

It's not uncommon for a person to reflect on their past ideas and change their mind. It's also not uncommon for a writer to turn transformative personal experiences into a work of fiction—setting opposing opinions against each other and letting readers work them out. Perhaps this is what Wouk did in writing *Caine*: carefully wrapping his preoccupations on the nature of leadership and duty in the guise of fiction.

And yet, more than a year before Wouk wrote his memo and nearly a decade before *Caine* was published, on another ocean, another story was writing itself.

The officers aboard the USS *Partridge*, a minesweeper built at the end of WWI and assigned mostly to towing and screening duties, faced a similar dilemma of choosing between a fallible leader and their duty to safeguard their ship. In a time of war, when death lurked beneath the waters around them, what could they do if they lost confidence in the man who possessed near-absolute power?

Before Wouk played out this dilemma with Queeg and Maryk and Willie Keith and Thomas Keefer, there was Adnah Caldin, Joe Cooney, Thomas Buffum, Frank Lefavor, Mike Rich, and Bill Ames. The central dramas of their stories are strikingly similar. And, in the end, their story travelled from the Atlantic to the Pacific and ultimately to Okinawa, where Herman Wouk's *Southard* sat stranded on a coral reef.

Maybe Wouk's ambiguity about Queeg was a lingering thought that he was based on someone real. Not just a sketched villain based on the drunken proclamations of junior officers, but an actual captain who lost control of his ship, told to him by a decorated officer just transferred from the North Atlantic.

They would have most likely met around Buckner Bay in Okinawa and Wouk would have heard stories about a captain driving his crew to the brink of mutiny, incompetence under pressure, and, eventually, a formal hearing. And Wouk would have heard it all from Lt. Thomas Buffum, formerly the executive officer of the *USS Partridge*.

Chapter 3
War in Paradise

In July of 1941, the German Wehrmacht was poised to take Moscow, the British were being pushed back in North Africa, the Japanese were preparing to attack Pearl Harbor, and Ensign White needed a haircut. He had just reported for duty aboard the USS *Partridge* which had recently set sail from Pearl Harbor and was headed toward the Panama Canal. White was settling into his role as an officer aboard a naval vessel. It was smaller than he anticipated. Before reporting for duty, he contemplated getting a haircut, but decided to wait until he was aboard. He had planned to visit the barber shop touted in many Navy recruiting brochures at the time along with a library, soda fountain, and a piano for sing-a-longs, but these were amenities of modern aircraft carriers, battleships, and destroyers. They were comforts unheard of on the ancient Bird Boat. Instead, the young ensign, a "90-day wonder" from San Diego, had to make due with a wooden folding chair set on the aft deck of an antiquated minesweeper, sailing through the Pacific Ocean. Over him, stainless-steel scissors glistening in the sun, was Floyd Pedersen, the ship's "barber."

It was White's first haircut at sea and, if the swelling ocean and lurching deck made him nervous, knowing it was also a first for Pedersen would have been little comfort. Pedersen, strictly speaking, wasn't even trained to cut hair. A sometime actor, sometime stagehand, Pedersen learned to cut hair backstage in theaters throughout Southern California. But this was the USS *Partridge* in 1941, and knowing a little of something made you an expert.

A few months earlier, Pedersen had begun his full-time career in the Navy. He had short acting stints in Los Angeles and worked regularly at the city's Grove Theater. He even had a brush with greatness, double-dating with Robert Mitchum, Larain Day, and Julie Mitchum.

But the work had dried up, and he needed something new. By early 1940, he figured that if he wasn't a star in the theater by now, he'd never be. He wanted to get into the radio business and had heard the Navy could train him. Being technically inclined, Pedersen did what many young men did in an America still recovering from 10 years of economic depression— he joined the Navy.

Reporting aboard the *Partridge* in San Diego, Pedersen found that, while his eagerness to learn all there was to learn about radio was appreciated, the skills he acquired backstage were more valuable to Captain S. E. Kenney. The ship needed a barber and Pedersen had, at one time, cut hair. After setting sail, his first customer was a new officer, fresh from the academy, named Jim White.

Ensign White would gain a reputation with the crew for his even temper, fairness, and the ability to be both friendly with his men and a good leader. By official Navy standards, White would have been considered too familiar with the enlisted men, but his leadership suited a Lapwing boat. Formalities broke down on these small ships and "Sail Easy" Kenney's approach to command permeated through to the ship's youngest officers, including White.

This style of leadership became crucial to the command of a small ship like the *Partridge,* particularly with an influx of inexperienced officers and crew. Trust between the officers and crew grew during their daily interactions and was later tested in combat. In one telling incident, Pedersen spotted Ensign White sitting with another officer at a watering hole on St. Thomas. White called him over and asked if he was returning to the *Partridge.* Pedersen said he was and White handed him his wallet. He didn't want to chance losing it or getting jumped later that night. The next day at roll call, Pedersen handed the wallet back to White, who stuck it in his pocket without counting the contents. Sixty-five years later, Pedersen recalled this episode as the kind of small gesture that built respect between White and the crew.

But on the aft deck, giving his first Navy haircut, Floyd Pedersen didn't know anything about Ensign White. Command at sea was absolute, and a bad haircut could have spelled the end to Pedersen's prized assignment on the radio in the bridge. Taking a deep breath, the actor turned sailor turned barber began to make his cuts. The ship tossed so badly, however, that it was impossible to keep anything straight. As things got worse, Pedersen decided to come clean.

"Mr. White, I'm sorry, but I can't make a straight cut in this water."

The young officer took a look in the mirror at his hacked-up but closely cropped hair.

"It's OK. We're not going to be in Panama for another 14 days."

The Partridge crosses through the Panama in 1941

Pedersen learned what the rest of the crew would learn throughout the coming war. White valued honesty and effort over ego and perfection. The sailors would reach out to him in their darkest hour, when his style of leadership was sorely needed.

The *Partridge* arrived in the Caribbean via the Panama Canal in late July of 1941. It was her first voyage into the Atlantic in almost 20 years. Commanding at her bridge was Lt. Cmdr. S.E. "Sail Easy" Kenney, her captain, and Executive Officer Boatswain P.S. Nystrom—both typical of Navy professionals between the wars. They were tough, experienced men whose careers had little chance to grow in a threadbare peacetime Navy. But they were driven by tradition and a love of life at sea.

*Floyd Pedersen who worked as an actor in Hollywood
before serving aboard the Partridge*

Kenney, the *Partridge's* skipper from 1939 to 1943, was genuinely old enough to earn the affectionate name of "the old man"—a nickname often given to captains half his age later in the war. In his mid-fifties when the war broke out, Kenney commanded sailors decades younger than himself. This age difference was, until 1942, the typical relationship between sea captains and their crew. Expertise in navigation, maneuvers, weather patterns, Navy protocols, and even the complex relationships between officers and crew traditionally required someone with years of experience and unquestionable authority at the helm.

Sailing through the Panama Canal, Kenney took his place in a wide captain's chair, a cigar dangling from his mouth at a peculiar angle due to his severe overbite, watching keenly over the pilot house and across the water. If there were doubts in his mind about the readiness of his ship and its crew to face a formidable enemy, Kenney hid them beneath a mask of unwavering confidence and calm. Like many good commanders, the war didn't change Kenney; he was a Navy man who took its challenges in stride and helped to create a competent team of officers and crew that could prevail in any situation no matter the adversity. And, in the coming war, the Navy would need that team.

The Navy was traditionally more selective than other branches of the military in terms of both physical fitness and education, requiring all men to have graduated from high school or have some kind of equivalent degree (only about 20 percent of the total population had a high school degree in 1940). Even though there was a surge of new recruits after the attack on Pearl Harbor, volunteer enlistment eventually waned and competition between services over the nation's pool of healthy, educated young men grew fierce. General Hershey, who served as the Executive Officer of the Selective Services from 1936 to 1970, characterized recruitment campaigns from all branches of the service as "ruthless." Early in 1942, Selective Services terminated an agreement to give the Navy lists of 1-A classified names and, by the middle of 1942, it became clear that the Navy would have to depend, at least in part, on the draft to supply its growing need for manpower.

For better or for worse, this meant that captains like "Sail Easy" Kenney would be dealing with a flood of new recruits who were younger, less experienced, and less educated than the modern Navy had ever accepted into its ranks. Many new sailors found themselves aboard the *Partridge* after just three weeks of training, with only the basic skills needed to work in an engine room, man guns, or serve as lookouts. For most, it was their first time at sea and, for many 17-, 18-, and 19-year-olds, it was their first time away from home. Some could not even swim.

Kenney did not just settle for what he had; he set out to shape and mold young recruits through a combination of discipline and education. The *Partridge's* logs from these years reveal plenty of punishments doled out for disorderly conduct, sailors absent over leave, and drunkenness. However, Kenney also appointed himself Education Officer, taking new recruits under his wing to teach them basic skills of good seamanship. Bill Ames, a signalman and eventually chief quartermaster, remembered the old man squinting up at a Planter's Peanut can that he held in an outstretched hand to show the ship's relationship with the stars and demonstrate how celestial navigation worked. Reading charts, working lines, navigating channels: these were skills that readied a crew for the unpredictable situations they would face. Getting this education directly from a ship's commanding officer was a rare privilege for the newly minted sailors. Many had transferred from larger ships where the captains were distant figures of authority who shaped the ship's command but with whom everyday contact was rare.

Under Kenney, men aboard the *Partridge* gained what some of later generations would seek in colleges and universities. They learned to think independently, seek out challenges, and grow into adults. They learned how to navigate without radar, how to keep engines running that were older than they were, how to barter with local suppliers to get the best grub and find the right places to get drunk on warm Caribbean nights. They also learned how to improvise in an early-war Navy that provided less than adequate supplies, technology, and trained men.

Men aboard the *Partridge* kept repair planks on the deck of the ship so that, if she sank, debris would be available for life rafts. They learned submarine hot spots. They learned from experienced tugboat crews that towlines had to be let out at exactly the right length to avoid snags on the bottom of the sea. And they learned a thousand other skills, tricks, and shortcuts that would make their survival possible—things the naval code did not and could not cover. They made it up as they went along because there was no alternative.

Captain Kenney and later Captain Snipes were able to see the value of youthful inexperience and tap into it. These commanders did not ride herd over a rabble—they brought out the best in everyday boys from all over America.

Many of these sailors were like my grandfather, Thurman Krouse, who joined the Navy with only a ninth grade education and had rarely traveled from rural Maryland. With a calm demeanor and a quiet personality, he earned the name "Thermostat" from his shipmates. In Depression-era America, the 19-year-old could have probably found work in the tomato fields around his hometown of Chewsville or possibly as a mechanic's assistant. Instead, he found himself, like many of his shipmates, plunged into the bureaucracy of the military as well as the time-honored Naval codes, traditions, and technologies that would have been, without the war, far from reach. He also found a place for his natural mechanical skill and curiosity to flourish, a development that would serve him for the rest of his life. And for a young man accustomed only to small town

America, the azure waters of the Caribbean were a magical vision that lingered in memory for decades.

Bill Ames, who had previously served aboard the USS *Wasp*, a carrier with some 2,100 officers and crew, learned navigation and signaling directly from Kenney—skills he would later use to escape German subs and guide the *Partridge* to safety. Floyd Pedersen, the actor-turned-barber, eventually did make it to the bridge as the ship's main radio operator. Thomas Buffum, a young "90-day wonder," transformed into a capable leader, keeping men together and alive during the ship's darkest hour. Frank Lefavor, an engineering officer, moved up to be a line officer during this period, learning the ins and outs of navigation, communication, and commanding men. Kenney looked for the potential in young men put aboard his ship and built on it, no matter how slight.

At times, this transformation wasn't easy. Many of the newly arrived were given the simplest of duties to build their skills and confidence. Serving lookout on the flying bridge just above the pilot house was one of the quickest ways to train a man in Navy jargon and the overall operation of the ship. Bill Ames recalled one sailor, arriving from the hills of Appalachia, who claimed to be able to carve a perfect crescent on an outhouse door and often replaced "Land Ho!" and "Ship Ahoy!" with his own unique phrases. When the country boy turned Navy man called out "Ship Ahoy!" the quartermaster replied "Where Away!" A correct response of "One point off the starboard bow!" or "One point to the port beam!" would have been appropriate. Instead, a response of "Over Yonder!" sailed back. Kenney's ever-present cigar fell from his mouth like a vaudeville prop. The mountain boy was strongly reprimanded.

Kenney's career and, indeed, the outcome of the war were now hanging in the balance with country boys, street kids, and college students—citizen sailors who were willing to sacrifice for their country, but were chipping away at the sometimes archaic Navy traditions that had always run a little deeper than those in other branches of the military. His patience and knowledge began to shape old Navy salts and fresh-faced recruits alike into an effective, efficient wartime crew that made the *Partridge* one of the most active ships in the Caribbean.

As the average age of the crew grew younger, it seemed to accentuate the age of the *Partridge* itself. And her main duties, never all that glamorous to begin with, presented an eager young recruit with plenty of mundane, work-a-day tasks.

The Navy in the early 1940s presented an exciting prospect for a young man. The latest technology was at his fingertips. Massive battleships and aircraft carriers were being constructed, destroyers cut through the water armed with sophisticated firing computers, and a fleet of submarines plied the depths of the sea.

And for all the danger and adventure the Navy presented, it also promised to keep young men "out of the trenches"—a memory that still loomed large in the minds of their parents, haunted by the Great War. Navy recruiting brochures may have boasted of modern onboard conveniences, but the *Partridge* had none of these amenities. "An overgrown tugboat" was the first impression many had of her. "It was a ship you walked down into," remembered Bill Ames. Rust perpetually ate at her hull. Wally Dothage, who served aboard from 1942 to 1944, remembered scraping paint on the side of the ship and punching directly through. Her only armament was two 3-inch/50 caliber guns and four 20mm guns plus two depth charge racks hastily added when the U-boat attacks ramped up toward the middle of 1942. The engine and steering systems were arcane and in constant need of repair. As if to punctuate its age, the anachronistic sail, a symbol of another era, was still mounted ready to unfurl on her aft deck. Dothage captured some of her grandeur in a poem he wrote:

> Its hull is thin and caked with rust,
> The instruments are old and filled with dust;
> Its gear is broken and beyond repair,
> To climb its mast, no one would dare.
> The decks are stained with oil and paint,
> Scrubbing and scraping is the deck hand's
>   complaint;
> The lines are old and filled with kinks,
> The chains are rusted in all the links.
> We work all day, and we stand watch all night,
> How do they expect us to keep up the fight?
> When our eyes are filled with dust and with dirt,
> We still are expected to keep on alert

The poem goes on to berate a lazy boatswain's mate and "yard birds" and "twidgets" who "lie in the sun and wait for their stew." It ends on a note of begrudging affection:

> But she is a good ship—and a working ship too,
> And she always manages to have something to do;
> She works awhile here and she works awhile
>   there,
> And she growls all the time like a damned old bear.

This was not the Navy of firing computers and sonar; this was the working Navy. The men of the *Partridge* seemed to feel affection for her not despite her challenges and flaws but because of them.

Built initially for a crew of 60, the ship's ranks eventually swelled to well over 90 men, making her small interior that much more cramped. The close quarters, however, brought the crew together rather than breeding tension and conflict. Men who served aboard the ship describe the crew as tight-knit from the officers to the stewards. Floyd Pedersen first thought serving aboard such a small ship might be a challenge, but soon found himself welcomed as an old friend. Joe Shannon, a young sailor from Boston, described the crew as a kind of family that he never had at home.

"My father had disappeared one day and we found out later he joined the Navy," recalled Shannon. "My brother and I joked that we joined up to find him and kick his ass."

As it turned out, Joe did find a family and father-figure in the *Partridge* in the Caribbean and beyond.

Many, whether serving on just a few ships during the war or on many ships over long careers at sea, described their *Partridge* experience as their best in the Navy.

On the *Partridge,* new recruits learned the ropes from "old salts" who were typical of the *Partridge* crew aboard before the Navy began its wartime buildup. Rough-around-the-edges and accustomed to the back-breaking work and perils of crewing a small ship throughout the Pacific, these were men for whom the war was only a minor change in the routine of drudgery at sea and the delights of frequent ports of call.

For many of the new officers or higher-ranking crew, service on the *Partridge* blurred the lines of rank so important on aircraft carriers and destroyers. Officers served a multitude of roles and the crew performed the lowest to highest duties interchangeably.

The camaraderie aboard ship that extended up and down the ranks revealed itself in simple ways. At some point in the Caribbean, the entire crew—officers and enlisted men alike—leapt from the rusting rails and swam in the warm waters off the anchored hull of their Bird Boat. The memory of splashing, diving, and enjoying the luxury of the clear blue water stuck with many of the men well into old age. Floyd Pedersen remembered that only Kenney remained aboard, looking down on them. "You could just see that he wanted to be there in the water with us," he recalled. "I felt sorry for him."

It was in these warm blue waters that the crew heard about the attack on Pearl Harbor from Kenney.

"The bastards finally did it," he said through his clenched cigar. The waters of the Caribbean were as tranquil as ever that day, but they wouldn't be for long. War was coming to Paradise.

1942 - 'The Happy Time'

How long does a ship take to sink? The *Titanic* sunk in 2 hours and 40 minutes. The battleship USS *Maine* was more destroyed by an explosion than sunk. She disintegrated into Havana Harbor. The *Lusitania* sunk off the South Coast of Ireland 20 minutes after being torpedoed by a German submarine. But in each case, hundreds of small stories culminate in the one single moment when the last piece of the ship disappeared beneath the waves.

Like the unfolding of a story, a ship's beginning threads stretch back in time, but its end is fixed. A ship going down is the ultimate drama, propelling a story of men thrust into the inhospitable domain of the open sea. Lives lost, victims of hubris, greed, war, miscalculation or simply being in the wrong place at the wrong time.

For all its complexity, *Moby Dick* is, at its heart, the anatomy of a shipwreck. The threads of the novel converge when the *Pequod* sinks beneath the waves:

> *For an instant, the tranced boat's crew stood still; then turned. "The ship? Great God, where is the ship?" Soon they, through dim, bewildering mediums saw her sidelong fading phantom, as in the gaseous Fata Morgana; only the uppermost masts out of water; while fixed by infatuation, or fidelity, or fate, to their once lofty perches, the pagan harpooneers still maintained their sinking lookouts on the sea. And now, concentric circles seized the lone boat itself, and all its crew, and each floating oar, and every lance-pole, and spinning, animate and inanimate, all round and round in one vortex, carried the smallest chip of the Pequod out of sight.*

This moment came for the SS *Lihue* on February 26, 1942, at 9:37 in the morning, with the loud snap of a heavy towline attached to the USS *Partridge*. A shockwave shuddered through the *Partridge* and threw the ship forward in *Lihue's* wake. The tiny Navy vessel took evasive maneuvers to clear the massive freighter as she lifted into the air and then plunged beneath the blue waters of the Caribbean. It had taken nearly three days, but the torpedo fired by Korvettenkapitän Albrecht

Achilles, commander of the German submarine *U-161*, finally downed its target.

For most of the sailors watching from the deck of the *Partridge,* the sinking of the *Lihue* was their first taste of war. They had left Pearl Harbor in July 1941 and crossed through the Panama Canal into the Caribbean. The attack on Pearl Harbor took place just a few months later and it seemed as though they had narrowly escaped the real naval war. The war was distant. Oceans away. Blackouts had been instituted but not often enforced. There were reports of subs in the area, but these were dismissed as apparitions conjured up by boys too eager to experience their piece of the action.

The same balmy air and blue water that greets vacationers to the Caribbean today seduced many of the sailors who served in these waters during WWII. Several members of the *Partridge's* crew had served in the warm climates of Hawaii, the South Pacific, and California. But for the new recruits, crystal-clear water and sun in February were like a dreamland. Sure, there were occasional signs that there was a war, but they were distant and muted.

A sailor on night watch spotted dolphins swimming through glowing algae in the clear, placid water and sounded the alarm, mistaking the creatures for a spread of torpedoes. Smoking was prohibited on deck at night. There was talk of arming the ship with depth charges and jokes about tossing buckets of paint onto submarine periscopes to fool them into surfacing. But all in all, life was good in Paradise. But war eventually came, just the same as it did around world, and changed the lives forever for those in it.

It started with ships sinking up and down the Eastern Seaboard and the Caribbean. Dozens of ships torpedoed by German U-boats at an alarming rate. In the midst of this destruction, the *Partridge* was dispatched to rescue the *Lihue,* the first of many rescue and salvage operations. Along with a salvage crew placed aboard the vessel from the Canadian armed merchant cruiser HMCS *Prince Henry,* the *Partridge* crew worked hard to save the *Lihue.* For a while, it looked like she might make it to shore with her cargo intact, but after a three-day fight, she plunged beneath the waves.

The *Partridge* and her crew would see worse in the months to come. Pulling oil-covered survivors from the water, witnessing the carnage of torpedoed and shelled passenger ships docked in harbors, playing cat and mouse with U-boats—these were the events that shaped the crew as wartime sailors and cemented their trust in their captain, officers, and one another.

As the U.S. struggled to get a fighting Navy ready to meet the Japanese at Midway, the Caribbean fleet would fight German subs on a shoestring. Ships began to be torpedoed on a daily basis up and down the East Coast and the Navy and Coast Guard seemed unable to counter the threat. The British had gained valuable experience fighting U-boats and had proven tactics at the ready, but the U.S. Navy largely ignored them, focusing instead on the carrier tactics used to great effect by the Japanese in the attack on Pearl Harbor.

The best the stretched fleet could do was to salvage anything they could from sinking ships, if possible by towing them to safety. Sometimes there was little to be picked up but bodies floating in the water.

Germany's U-boat war brought the conflict closer to Americans than often recalled. Spectators up and down the East Coast would gather to watch ships burning in coastal waters. Citizens from New York City to Charleston awoke to explosions just offshore. Debris collected on beaches. Americans watched for periscopes and submarine profiles from concrete towers that still exist up and down the Eastern Seaboard.

And Germany's capacity to broaden its front against America's shipping lanes was expansive. Ships were attacked in South America, the Gulf of Mexico, throughout the Caribbean, up the Florida Keys, and all the way to New England. Germany's tactic was not just to terrorize the U.S. population and disrupt supplies to Europe—it was to stretch the U.S. Navy so thin it could not hope to win the war and America would be forced into a negotiated peace.

In his book *The U-boat War in the Caribbean,* Gaylord Kelshall called the Caribbean U-boat campaign "the most cost-effective campaign fought by Germany anywhere during World War II." Only 17 U-boats were sunk in the area, but for every U-boat sunk, the Allies lost 23.5 merchant ships. By 1942, 36 percent of all shipping losses worldwide occurred in the Caribbean. It was in this largely forgotten part of the war that the *Partridge* and her crew distinguished themselves. Operating in the blue waters of the Caribbean, they would find their mettle and define themselves as tough, resourceful, and up for anything.

In December 1941, British intelligence sent a detailed warning to Admiral Ernest King, Commander in Chief of the United States Fleet and Chief of Naval Operations. The warning outlined the strong possibility of a "heavy concentration of U-boats off the North American seaboard." Greeting this threat was a woefully inadequate coastal defense consisting of just seven Coast Guard cutters, four converted yachts, three 1919-vintage patrol boats, two gunboats dating to 1905, and four wooden submarine chasers. About 100 short-range aircraft, suitable only for training, were also available. No blackouts along the coast were enforced, and lighthouses and other navigational aids remained in operation, essentially guiding German submarines to their prey.

This was the opening salvo of *Operation Drumbeat*, a plan devised by Admiral Dönitz, commander of Germany's submarine force, to be a devastating second blow to America after the attack on Pearl Harbor. By the time it was contained, *Drumbeat* and its Caribbean component, *Neuland,* would claim 609 ships, sending a total of 3.1 million tons to the bottom of the sea—roughly one-quarter of all shipping sunk by submarines during the entire war. Over 2 million tons were sunk in January and February of 1942 alone. Dönitz reported that his forces were often presented with too many targets to attack—a dozen ships silhouetted neatly on the horizon against blazing city skylines. At times, submarines simply ran out of torpedoes before they did targets.

For the *Partridge, Drumbeat* arrived in late February 1942 as a second wave of U-boats arrived in the Caribbean during *Drumbeat's* evolution, *Operation Neuland.* One of the subs was the *U-161,* commanded by Kapitänleutnant Albrecht Achilles, which would cross paths with the *Partridge* on more than one occasion.

Although the dangers of submarine warfare were great, at this point in the war Achilles sat in an enviable position. *U-161* was a product of Germany's many years of build-up to war. Modern, armed with the latest weaponry, and capable of striking at the U.S. without the need for at-sea refueling, *U-161* was one of the German Navy's long-range IX class U-boats.

This was Achilles' first combat mission as a commander. Leaving Lorient on the Brittany coast of

France on January 24, 1942, he sailed the *U-161* with a convoy of subs all part of *Operation Neuland*. Before the war, Achilles had served as a cadet officer with the Hamburg America merchant ship line through the Caribbean and knew its waters well. Gaylord Kelshall described how Achilles' experience aided the young U-boat captain in navigating the tight dangerous passages in the Caribbean like the Bocas, a small chain of islands between Trinidad and Venezuela:

> *"Achilles had not only entered the Bocas many times but had also done quite a lot of sailing in the harbour and among the islands. Prior to the war, local residents had always watched the Hamburg America ships with awe, because of the speed at which they always transited the Bocas. Most vessels took great care when slowly penetrating the rock-strewn area, but the German ships had been known as the only ones which seemed not to care for a slow careful entry. Now a former Hamburg America man was going to enter the heavily guarded Bocas on a mission to destroy."*

On February 19, 1942, Achilles made a daring maneuver into the harbor of Port of Spain, Trinidad. After evading land and sea patrols by resting the *U-161* on the seabed, Achilles torpedoed the U.S. merchant ship *Mokihana* at the entrance of the harbor and the steam tanker *British Consul* anchored there. Although both ships were later salvaged (the *Partridge* towed the *Mokihana* back to the U.S. several months later), they were registered as kills because all cargo was lost. The *Mokihana* had a hole opened 35 feet by 45 feet on her starboard side just forward of the bridge, and would have been a complete loss had she not sunk in such shallow water. When she was torpedoed, the *Mokihana* had all her anchor, cargo, and port lights burning and was silhouetted against the lights onshore. In addition, the Allied response was slow and uncoordinated, leaving Achilles plenty of time to escape. In fact, the sub passed directly under shore batteries with her running lights on. Sentries were simply not expecting to see a U-boat so close to shore operating with such freedom in the heavily guarded area. The "Happy Time," as the Germans referred to this bonanza of sinking, lived up to its name for Achilles. But his first patrol revealed the true risks and ugly realities of undersea warfare.

J.P. Morgan's yacht Corsair IV viewed through the damaged hull of the Mokihana.

In the early morning hours of February 23, 1942, *U-161* surfaced near the SS *Lihue*, a seven-ton cargo ship that had been crippled by one of its torpedoes fired 15 minutes before. Achilles most likely watched the ship for signs of her sinking and calculated that a few well-planted shots from the sub's deck gun would finish her off without expending an additional torpedo. Targets were plentiful and a saved torpedo meant another chance to score a kill.

As Achilles surfaced the *U-161* and closed in on the *Lihue,* he sent crews to the deck, and commenced firing, expecting the large target to absorb their shots and sink beneath the waves. Instead, they were answered with a barrage of fire from the *Lihue's* three-inch gun as well as its four .50 caliber and two .30 caliber machine guns. The hail of fire in the increasingly bright morning sky forced Achilles to call the crew back, seal the hatches, and dive under fire.

The young sub captain was now wary of the ship he had just attacked. Was it a trap? Would she go under or begin circling the area dropping depth charges? Traps such as these were not unheard of. In fact, the *Partridge* would later escort a disguised tall ship from Bermuda to New York City. These Q-ships were fitted with a disguised U.S. Navy crew and concealed guns. A submarine spotting such as easy target would not waste torpedoes but would surface without fear of being rammed only to be met with a hail of gunfire and artillery from hidden weapons.

Today, Achilles was in no danger of such a trap, but cautiously decided to stay submerged, remain still, and wait. It is not known whether *U-161* stayed close by, watching to see if the ship was sinking, or if she ventured further afield only to return later. In any case, that evening at 6:39 PM the *Lihue* came under attack from *U-161* a second time—a testament to the free will exerted by the U-boats in the early days of the war. No Navy or Coast Guard ships patrolled the area and reconnaissance by air came hopelessly late. Achilles fired one torpedo, which the crippled ship managed to evade. A second was fired 15 minutes later. Whether due to the

Lihue's maneuvering or mistakes in firing, it missed its target as well.

Possibly suspecting the *Lihue* had an experienced naval crew aboard, Achilles withdrew from the attack, counting it as one that got away. In fact, he had scored the fatal blow to the ship with the first torpedo, but only the crew of the *Partridge* would see the final moments of the *Lihue* as she plunged beneath the waves.

Despite heroic efforts to evade attack and stay afloat, the *Lihue* was no longer capable of making way under her own power and was beginning to take on water. When British Tanker *British Governor* passed nearby, the captain ordered the ship to be abandoned. Later that day the *Lihue* was boarded by a salvage crew from the Canadian armed merchant cruiser HMCS *Prince Henry*.

Two days later, the *Partridge* arrived to find the *Lihue* badly damaged and in need of a tow. The crew would attempt to tow the ship to St. Lucia and a group of volunteers boarded and salvaged its machine guns, operated the pumps, and secured the tow lines. One of them was a young signalman named Bud Froehlich, who kept a journal of his time aboard the *Partridge*.

Froehlich had reported for duty to the *Partridge* along with Bill Ames from the USS *Wasp*. Life could scarcely be more different aboard the two vessels and their time together on the smaller ship cemented a friendship that continued for the rest of their lives.

On February 25, 1942, Froehlich recorded his efforts aboard the *Lihue*. Entering its cargo hold, the *Partridge* volunteers saw what was at stake in their salvage operation. The ship was a floating warehouse, filled with heavy equipment and other supplies. Froehlich recorded that the hold contained eight heavy bombers, about 20 Ford automobiles, and dozens of trucks; its decks were filled with aircraft engines. All told, the ship carried nearly 5,000 tons of cargo essential to the war effort.

The boarding crew had to work fast. Rigging the tow was not easy given the list of the ship and its sheer size. They were also keenly aware that the sub that had persistently attacked the *Lihue* might return to prey on the *Partridge.*

As a U.S. Army bomber circled overhead to provide cover, the crew worked with the Canadians still aboard to rig the ship for a tow and control the damage. The ship had to be rigged from the aft to prevent water from rushing in through its damaged hull and further straining the *Partridge's* triple reciprocating engine. To make matters worse, the weather turned, churning up the sea and tossing the massive cargo ship against the *Partridge.*

In the meantime, Kenney ordered the machine gun defenses to be removed from the *Lihue,* should the ship sink. After completing the rigging, the *Partridge* crew was ordered back and the ship pushed full speed ahead. Straining against the tow line, she managed to make just under two knots. Ominously, the bomber escort that had been circling overhead left the scene. The meagerly armed *Partridge's* best hope for survival would be that her profile, at a distance, resembled a destroyer. Aside from this, she and the *Lihue* presented a large, slow-moving target.

That evening, the watch was quiet and the Caribbean Sea slowly drifted by under the growl of the *Partridge's* engines. Few appreciated the wisdom of Captain Kenney's decision to call back his crew. For even as they spoke, sharing jokes and trading stories about the day, the *Lihue* shifted and began to list from her port side. It was the beginning of the end.

In the morning, Kenney, White, and Froehlich stood on the bridge eyeing the new list on the tow. Kenney shook his head, knowing that the *Lihue* was doomed. Without warning, the *Lihue's* stern began to lift out of the water. The captain quickly shifted the *Partridge* astern as the massive ship rose in the air, hung there for a moment, and then plunged beneath the waves. As the towline snapped under the pressure, a shock wave shot through the *Partridge,* followed by a massive wave from the *Lihue's* plunge into the deep. It was all over in a matter of seconds.

The USS Partridge towing the stricken Mokihana
in the Caribbean in 1942 off Trinidad.

This time, no one had been hurt or killed, the *Lihue* sinking simply added to the growing tonnage sent to the bottom of the sea by German wolf packs during America's first year at war. For the *Partridge*, however, the episode was a proving ground for the strength of the ship as well as its command.

It was the first time, during war, that Kenney saw his crew perform. Swift, decisive, and—save for the looting of a few candy bars—professional, they were men to be proud of. The skills needed to rig such a large, unstable vessel would be applied again and again through the *Partridge's* tour of the Caribbean and would be essential in the ship's participation in the Normandy invasion.

By pulling his men off the *Lihue,* knowing it could sink in seconds, Kenney had cemented the crew's trust in him. No matter what, it was clear: "Sail Easy" had their best interests at heart.

For Albrecht Achilles, commander of the *U-161,* the incident was a pure failure. In the midst of a bonanza of confirmed kills, his four attacks on merchant ships had only produced only one confirmed kill. It was the *Circe Shell,* a British oil tanker sunk two days before the attack on the *Lihue.* So far the *Circe* also resulted in the only death inflicted by Achilles. All that would change in the waters of St. Vincent a week later.

Bud Froehlich's log notes reveal the peculiar war being fought in and around the hundreds of islands that rise out of the sea in a crescent from Florida to Puerto Rico, all the way around to Antigua and the coast of South America.

It's often been said that most warfare is hours, days, and weeks of monotony followed by seconds of terror. For a ship operating in submarine-infested waters on a daily basis, immediate danger was invisible and always near—and for a ship the size of the *Partridge,* a torpedo could mean total destruction instantly. The only safe place from them was in a harbor. And even then things weren't completely secure.

Shortly after the *Lihue* incident, the *Partridge* entered port at St. Lucia. Froehlich recorded in his diary a strange life of wartime in the Caribbean spent staring at the sea and sky for indications that the war was even happening. In between was paradise.

He wrote about bombing runs against subs in the distance and excursions to pick up U-boat attack survivors. But there were also sandy beaches for swimming, palm trees for climbing, baseball games, and cookouts. And there was a constant refrain in the *Partridge's* logs: scraping rust and painting.

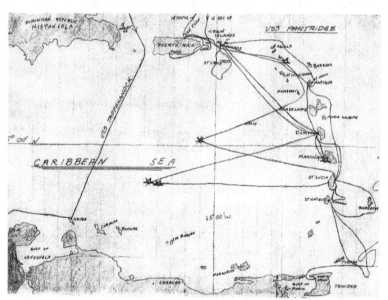

A page from Bud Froehlich's wartime journal

Bud Froehlich and Bill Ames in the Caribbean
while serving together aboard the Partridge

Froehlich's log from March 6 reveals how closely danger lurked, even as the backdrop of war became increasingly normal to the men aboard. After the crew lost a baseball game to a group of Marines at the St. Lucia airbase (13 to 5—he notes that "they had a good field and team but we were all out of practice"), the *Partridge* was ordered to proceed 50 miles out to sea to pick up survivors from the torpedoed SS *Uniwaleco*.

While the *Lihue* incident had been a valuable learning experience for the *Partridge* crew, the *Uniwaleco* would be its first introduction into the horrors of modern naval warfare.

The *Partridge* searched the waters all night and found nothing of the ship, then pulled into St. Vincent to see if the crew had made it ashore. Some of the crew had landed on the island in lifeboats, but some were still missing. Soon, a lone lifeboat was spotted by a PBY Catalina flying boat, and the *Partridge* rushed to their position. Bud Froehlich wrote of what they found:

> *"I'll never forget the sight of those eight men, one man was dead, one was completely burnt, all had injuries."*

After bringing the injured and fatigued survivors aboard, the crew of the *Partridge* discovered what had happened during the previous two nights. The tanker *Uniwaleco* carrying a full load of gasoline was unescorted on the evening of March 7, 1942, when *U-161* found her. Achilles unleashed two torpedoes and scored a single hit. Forty-five miles west of St. Vincent, the *Uniwaleco* cruised out of control, turning in circles as the crew abandoned ship. All hands made it safely into lifeboats on both the port and starboard sides of the ship when disaster struck.

Maybe Achilles was still shaken by his experience with the *Lihue* and didn't want to risk surfacing to finish off the ship. Maybe he had become impatient for a confirmed kill. Maybe he didn't see the lifeboats and crew still climbing down the sides of their crippled ship, or maybe he did. He unleashed a second set of torpedoes directly between two of the lifeboats loading crew from the ship; the results were devastating.

The two lifeboats closest to the torpedo were smashed to pieces, killing everyone aboard immediately. The three remaining capsized, sending the crew into water filled with burning debris floating in thick oil. Flaming oil and gasoline sprayed into the air, searing skin on contact and burning victims even in the water. The *Uniwaleco* cracked in half and sank in less than three minutes, leaving the survivors alone in the water. The crew of *U-161* listened with fascination as the ship continued to explode on its journey to the bottom of the sea. The explosions were so intense, even at two miles away, that some thought the sub was under attack.

Captain Johannes Rosvik and the *Uniwaleco* crew, now helpless in the water, managed to right three of the lifeboats and proceeded to row toward Saint Vincent. Two of the boats made it ashore, but the other, with only eight men aboard, was too light to make it over the surf. The eight men struggled to keep the boat in sight of land but as their strength began to wane, they drifted farther out to sea.

By the time the *Partridge* picked up the survivors in this lifeboat, one had died from his injuries while the others were frozen in shock. After dropping off the remainder of the *Uniwaleco* crew in Kingstown harbor by 16:00, the *Partridge* proceeded to Antigua to serve as a submarine screening escort for a tug and dredge. By 23:00 their orders had changed. A smaller British tanker had been sunk near Trinidad. The *Partridge* was sent to pick up survivors. War, for Froehlich and his crewmates, had become much more than near misses and candy bars.

The hectic pace of the *Partridge's* missions in the early months of the war came to define the ship and her crew. During this period, the *Partridge* adopted its Donald Duck mascot. In all likelihood it was drawn by Donald Jaeger, a carpenter's mate from New York City. Joining the Navy after building PT boats in Bayonne, Jaeger had a knack for drawing cartoons and liked Disney characters most.

No one seemed to mind that it was the wrong bird; Jaeger's work was the right sentiment for the crew and their tough little ship. The *Partridge's* duck peers out with a confused, angry, and somewhat overwhelmed expression, overburdened by the depth charges and machine gun bullets slung across his shoulders. This is not the angry, fierce duck used widely in Army and Navy insignia throughout the war. Here, Donald is plump and startled, but ready for whatever is thrown its way; *"What Next?"* is the caption next to the befuddled bird.

Like many of the mascots adopted during the war, the *Partridge's* embodied the peculiar American spirit of laughing in the face of your own shortcomings. Their ship was no sleek, fighting machine with a crack professional crew. They were mostly boys, out of their element on a ship built for another time and another purpose, but together they had met the challenges of the opening days of the war and responded by saying: *What Next?*

What Next? could have easily been the motto for Bill Ames but with an entirely different tone. His upbeat demeanor, exuberance in the face of mundane duty, and sheer perseverance turned the bewildered, befuddled duck's question into a genuine question. What, Bill Ames would ask, was next?

The phrase passed through Ames' mind as he sat on a floating platform, trailing behind his ship. He was staring at a cheese sandwich he packed for lunch, or at least what was left of it. He had included pickles in the sandwich, but now the heat of the day had melted the cheese. The combination of pickle juice and melted cheese had turned his entire lunch into a soggy, hot mush. Still, sitting under the hot noon-day sun, hungry and smelling of pickles, was the least of his concerns.

Ames was sitting on top of the floating machine shop (FMS) being towed by the *Partridge*. The *Partridge* had picked up the FMS in Florida and progress had been slow down the Keys toward Trinidad, their final destination. The FMS was a vessel with some maneuvering power intended to lift engines out of ships for repair and retooling, eliminating the need for dry docking the entire ship. The new skipper, Lieutenant Rodney Snipes, had chosen Ames to go aboard during the tow and handle communication between the two vessels and to assist the FMS crew with maneuvering the unwieldy craft—it was never intended for a sea voyage and her crew had no experience.

It was dangerous enough to be aboard the *Partridge,* but now Ames was stuck on what amounted to a slow-moving target for any sub they happened upon. Pickle juice aside, this was a dangerous mission. But it was also a tremendous honor. The skipper had chosen him over the Chief Quartermaster for the assignment and so it took on a feeling of special importance for the sailor—both an honor and a test.

Part of the reason Ames' role was so important was the radio silence that had to be kept between the two craft. Any chatter would give away their position to subs operating in the area.

Ames knew that scanning the horizon for periscopes was probably hopeless. Still, it felt like the most active thing to be doing and made him feel that he had some power over the situation. In any case, the horizon was empty—just blue water and blue sky, accompanied by the constant drone of the ship's engines. Then Ames spotted a plane.

At first, it was just a dot on the horizon. Gradually, the buzzing from its engines came within earshot and the plane headed for the *Partridge* and swooped in low. It was a Coast Guard bomber patrolling for submarines and it was flashing a message. Ames shaded his eyes and squinted to read the flashes against the bright sunlit sky. He could just barely make it out and the news wasn't good. Ahead, only a few miles near Martinique and directly on the *Partridge's* course, lay a pack of U-boats.

Not knowing whether or not the *Partridge* had received the message, Ames sprang into action. He pulled out a navigation chart to plot the *Partridge's* position, the subs' position according to the bomber, and possible alternative routes—all skills he could trace to Kenney's education. (Although Kenney had left the *Partridge* a month earlier, Captain Snipes seemed to take an interest in Ames' continual development.)

Ames signaled a recommendation for a change of course around Martinique, maintaining radio silence. Using one of the islands as a shield was their best chance. A course adjustment to the south would cut off the subs and give the *Partridge* a safe passage to Trinidad.

Captain Snipes received the message and ordered a change in course. That night, the two vessels maintained a total signal blackout. In the distance, U-boats sent up distress flares, hoping the *Partridge* would reveal her location. Ames' quick thinking paid off—the ship and her tow sailed into Trinidad the next day. Back on board, Ames was called into Captain Snipes' wardroom.

Two glasses of whiskey sat on the desk. The captain offered Ames a seat and lifted a glass to him as a gesture of congratulations.

Puzzled, Ames assumed the Captain knew it was his birthday and thanked him. Snipes poured another.

"That was for your birthday. This one's for your promotion."

Snipes had put in for promotion to Chief Quartermaster. After several refusals based on his age, the promotion had been approved. Ames was now the youngest sailor of that rank in the Navy.

If Kenney was the skipper that taught sailors the basics of navigating the sea, Snipes seemed to impart the basics of fighting a war. It was during Snipes' brief time in command that a group of *Partridge* men set ashore in a rare and completely unauthorized combat mission. As losses mounted throughout the Caribbean, frustration grew at the unseen enemy that would appear from nowhere, strike, and sink beneath the waves. To make matters worse, the Germans sought refuge on the islands colonized by countries they occupied in Europe.

Island politics often brought diplomatic confusion to the chaos of war. Once, the *Partridge* ran afoul of the Cuban government when the ship made an unauthorized excursion into a shallow harbor to seek refuge from a German sub attack. Worried its cargo ships would be targeted in retaliation for harboring U.S. vessels, the Cubans detained the *Partridge,* releasing the ship only after two days of negotiations with the U.S. Embassy in Havana.

The crew of the *Partridge* took matters into their own hands when it came to dealing with Martinique. Martinique was controlled by Vichy France, the supposedly free and unoccupied portion of France after the country was invaded by Germany. And while the island was not technically in control of the Germans, its loyalty was always uncertain. A treaty actually existed between the Vichy government on Martinique and the United States prohibiting naval operations and assisting in the U-boat war. But in February of 1942, an injured German officer from *U-156* had his leg amputated at the French Military hospital. After his recovery, he took an active role in the affairs of the island. Around this time, the crew of the *Partridge* began to pick up radio messages from the island to German subs, aiding them in locating ships and convoys. Transmissions were broadcast uncoded and, on more than one occasion, the crew heard the *Partridge* named in target lists for upcoming attacks.

The *Partridge* had been one of the ships targeted in an attack by Achilles' *U-161* on Port Castries and was actually erroneously reported by the Germans as being sunk there. The ship had actually left the port a day earlier. The British ship *Untata* and the Canadian transport *Lady Nelson* were not so fortunate. They were sunk in the same docks where the *Partridge* had been moored just days before.

Achilles' attack on Port Castries was a bold, almost reckless move. A narrow channel twists and turns its way into its harbor and is too shallow for a U-boat to dive. Posting lookouts on the conning tower, Achilles maneuvered his ship in semi-moonlight past sentries at the entrance to the harbor, fired two torpedoes at the *Lady Nelson* and *Untata,* then hastily retreated under machine gun fire.

The attack on Port Castries was devastating. In addition to the two 8,000-ton ships sunk into the mud, much of the town, which extends down to the water, was severely damaged. Froehlich wrote of seeing the wreck of *Lady Nelson* only a few days later:

> *"We were tied alongside her and the stench was awful. Her stern was just a tangled mess. Two of the victims were still in the debris."*

It seemed as if there was little they could do but sit and listen to the broadcasts from Martinique and wonder if they would be next. Sitting and waiting, however, just wasn't in the nature of the hardscrabble *Partridge* crew; diplomats could argue about borders and sovereignty but, in the midst of the war at sea, things were less tidy.

Conducting a night exercise early in 1943, the *Partridge* dropped anchor off the coast of Martinique on a moonless night. A half dozen men slipped into the ship's dinghy, armed with rifles, and made their way to shore. Shots rang out and it was quickly over. The men made their way back to the *Partridge,* which fired its engines and slipped back into the night.

The incident doesn't exist in the ship's log and there is no official record of what happened on shore. But accounts from the crew are clear: six men from the *Partridge* ambushed the German radio outpost, killing its crew and destroying the equipment. It was an open secret aboard the ship and, afterward, a feeling of elation swept over the crew who knew about the mission. They had done their small part to fight back against the sub menace from Martinique until the island surrendered to Allied forces several months later.

In comparison with thousands of other brave acts throughout the war, the *Partridge's* night raid is little more than a footnote. But the attack that shattered a quiet Caribbean night demonstrated the initiative of the crew that Kenney shaped and Snipes fostered. It was the same crew that a new captain would inherit in December of 1943.

Chapter 4
Inheriting *Caine*

In time of peace some wait and prepare for many years before command comes. But in time of war some find themselves thrust into command almost before they feel equipped to its burdens.

— from Captain Harley F. Cope
Command at Sea, 1943

Late in 1943, Bill Ames was called into the Captain's wardroom again. Snipes got right to the point: he was being transferred off the *Partridge* to a new command, a newly commissioned ship out of Charleston, the USS *Chowanoc*. She was another small ship, but modern, newly built, and slated for action in the Pacific. Snipes could choose one sailor to transfer with him. He asked Ames if he wanted to go.

It was an appealing offer—an opportunity to shake down a new ship along with the prospect of serving with a captain he knew and liked. But Snipes leaned in and confided another piece of information. He had heard of the *Partridge's* new skipper; he had a reputation. Snipes warned Ames that he might not find life under his new command so easy.

Ames had grown to like life aboard the *Partridge* and enjoyed many of the benefits of serving as chief quartermaster, including having a private cabin, private dining, and other perks. But it was Snipes' bit of gossip that helped Ames to make his decision: he would stay. If things were going to get rough aboard the *Partridge,* he wanted to be there for the other guys. With all that was to come, it was a decision he never regretted.

Shortly afterward, the *Partridge* set sail for Norfolk, Virginia, arriving in November 1943. Refurbishments began on the vessel in dry-dock to ready her for a mission across the Atlantic.

In December, a new ensign, fresh from officers' training and a recent graduate of St. Vincent's College, reported for duty. Only four years earlier, Mike Rich had been a popular freshman, tooling around campus in his '29 Model A Ford. At the start of the war his education was put on a fast track and he began attending classes year-round. In February 1943 he graduated and accepted a commission in the Navy.

His first impression of the *Partridge* echoed Bill Ames: it wasn't a ship you walked up a gangplank to; you climbed down a ladder into it. Its passageways and cabins were crowded with officers and sailors—a full third more than it was originally intended to hold. He found his cabin with a bunk under construction to accommodate two officers. His cabin mate was another relatively new officer in the Navy as well. Joe Cooney, however, was entering it as a veteran sailor from WWI, an experienced ferry and tugboat captain, and a man twice the age of many of the officers and crew, including Rich.

Jim White at Guantanamo Bay, Cuba, 1943

Another big change for the *Partridge* at the end of 1943 was the departure of Jim White, the ensign who had been so forgiving of his bad haircut in rough seas. Now a lieutenant, White was taking command of the *Owl*, a ship in the same class as the *Partridge,* departing Norfolk for the U.K. on the same mission. White had actually traveled to Washington to protest the transfer, but was denied. In any case, he wouldn't be far from the men of the *Partridge* and their paths would cross again. For now, though, it was time to say goodbye.

When Herman Wouk's Willie Keith boards the *Caine*, his dreams of glory dissipate the moment he lays eyes on the dilapidated minesweeper, and things go from bad to worse when he meets the crew and his fellow officers. In one wardroom exchange, Tom Keefer, the ship's novelist-sailor, refers to the biblical implications of the ship's name.

"This ship is an outcast, manned by outcasts, and named for the greatest outcast of mankind. My destiny is the Caine. It's the purgatory for my sins."

And as Captain DeVries leaves the *Caine's* command, the crew presents him with a watch. In thanks, he says:

"I'll always keep it a half an hour slow...to remind me of the fouled-up crew of the Caine."

Cynicism permeates the men of *Caine*. Life aboard the ship is mundane, with no chance for glory—the kind of assignment everyone wants to avoid. *Caine* is troubled before Captain Queeg steps aboard: an undisciplined crew, more than one disgruntled officer, and aging, dilapidated equipment. Queeg invokes these facts several times to justify his strict discipline. Queeg may have been paranoid, incompetent, and cowardly, but he was correct, to some degree, about conditions aboard the *Caine*.

The *Partridge* offered a different challenge to a new captain looking to change the nature of its command. Rather than undisciplined and disgruntled, the men aboard the *Partridge* were an extremely close-knit, self-sufficient crew, who, for the most part, chose to stay aboard the ship over other assignments.

In Wouk's fiction, Queeg inherits a crew of malcontents and misfits with lax discipline and spotty adherence to naval code. If Queeg stepped aboard the *Partridge* instead of the *Caine,* he would have found a young, ambitious crew, eager to please and proud of their accomplishments. They may have been rough-around-the-edges, but they were far from discontent.

Queeg, however, did not step aboard the *Partridge.* In December of 1943, Captain Snipes said his farewells and turned over his command to Lt. Adnah Neyhart Caldin, a career Navy man who had served during WWI, done a stint in the merchant marine, and returned to the Navy as a professional career. Caldin was eager to become a commanding officer. The Navy offered him that opportunity as a necessity of war. In his view, the years of service he put in during peacetime paid dividends in the war. He had fought hard for what he had and would fight harder to keep it.

Caldin was stern and by-the-book and firmly believed in asserting his command every chance he got. Staring at officers over the tops of his wire-framed glasses with a look of a distrusting school teacher, he sent a clear message: he wasn't aboard to make friends. Demeanor aside, Caldin's experience spoke for itself. Caldin may not have been the friendliest of captains, but he was a professional. Some aboard may have even welcomed tighter discipline for a change.

Whether Caldin had been placed in command of the *Partridge* with a purpose is unknown, but his style of command could have been perceived as ideal for the ship's upcoming mission. His strict discipline, respect for the Navy way, and experience in the merchant marine all were ideal characteristics for the complex towing maneuvers to take place between Britain and France during the upcoming D-Day invasion.

The *Partridge* in the winter of 1943-44 was sailing into a new kind of war. The cavalier tactics she had employed while darting around the island backwaters of the war may have been suitable at that time and place. But the Navy was preparing for an amphibious assault on Fortress Europe—one that would need tight coordination among thousands of ships and millions of men. Caldin's leadership style, at least in theory, should have been well suited for the mission.

Chapter 5
The New Captain

The year 1944 was a time of change for Adnah Caldin. He said good-bye to his six-year-old daughter Lucy and his wife, Louise, just 10 days before Christmas. It was a small sacrifice for what he felt would be the opportunity he had longed for since he entered the Navy in the Great War. After so many years, he would finally have a chance to become a commissioned officer in the United States Navy. The ship was small, and lacked cutting-edge technology, but it was a command.

Indeed, command of a vessel, no matter how small, was a major milestone for any naval officer. And maybe more so for a man who had spent most of his adult life running from a small town with no future. If Caldin played his cards right, this command would be a foothold into the higher ranks of the Navy, where his rating of lieutenant might become permanent, giving him a shot at retiring after the war as a Lt. Commander, Commander, or even Captain. That would mean more money and prestige—a different life after the war. A different life for his wife and daughter. A different life from where he had started.

Caldin would be commanding a ship in a convoy sailing toward a major combat zone: the North Atlantic and English Channel. Towing targets and salvaging ships may have been the pride of the *Partridge* crew in the past, but now she was going to be part of the largest armada ever assembled, playing a pivotal role in its success. Sailing through the English Channel, she would report for duty in the crowded ports of Britain. It was a transition that the crew and officers of the ship would have to make, whether they were ready or not. And Caldin was the man to make them ready.

That winter may have been pivotal in Caldin's career, but the month marked a rough start for Joe Cooney. He was sick with a cold and exhausted by lack of sleep. The ship had undergone extensive repairs while docked in Norfolk and noise from the round the clock repair work made sleep inside the ship all but impossible. Wide-eyed recruits joined the Navy to see the world with eager, nervous enthusiasm. Joe Cooney was too old for all that. He wanted to get this job done and go home.

And punctuating his headache was the knowledge that his captain was almost certainly going to be a pain in the ass. Caldin's reputation preceded his arrival. The guys spread rumors that the old man was a real asshole, though Joe toned down that language in a letter to his wife Florie. He was a real 'doozie' in that letter. But Joe knew the drill. You always got someone in charge that puffed themselves up a little. Let the power go to their head. Sometimes those guys got results. Knock a few heads around and suddenly you have a nice tight ship.

It wasn't anything he hadn't seen before. He saw captains push a crew to the brink and then pull them back. Sure they'd bitch and moan, but you could see the respect in their eyes. Or not. It didn't matter. She was a tough ship. She'd float through anything. But that was all before Cooney met and served under Adnah Caldin.

On Wednesday, November 18, 1943, Cooney collapsed in his cabin aboard the *Partridge*. He had arrived on board at 7 AM that morning after a grueling 18-hour train ride from New York City. It wasn't until evening that he could finally retire to his cabin. But even the small luxury of sleep was denied the exhausted boatswain—the bangs, clatters, and grinding from work on the ship kept him wide awake. Cooney mixed himself a rum and coke and wrote a letter home to Florie back in Staten Island.

> *"There have been a lot of changes here in the past week. Our captain is being transferred to a new ship and Mr. White goes on a new ship too. It's hard to say what's going to happen before we get through. Mr. White is down in Washington now trying to change it. He wants to stay here with me or maybe he will get me transferred with him. I hope so."*

Cooney's attitude toward Jim White was typical of many of the crew and officers aboard the *Partridge*. Even 65 years later, they expressed unabashed affection for White as a fair-minded junior officer that may have been a "90-day wonder" but earned the respect of new recruits. And the feeling was clearly mutual, given White's trip to DC.

But while a close, family-like relationship may have been a positive experience for many aboard the *Partridge,* it was neither a priority nor a desirable situation for the Navy. One of the cruel facts of military command dictates that a commanding officer and particularly a captain cannot have a close relationship with his crew or his junior officers. The trust built during

White's tenure as an ensign and then lieutenant would have to be cast aside as he took command of his own ship, the USS *Owl,* commanded, at that point, by a Lt. Adnah Caldin. Special trip to DC or not, the Navy was not likely to consider White's request to stay. A close relationship with the officers and crew of a ship was all the more reason for the transfer.

There may have been nothing unusual about White's transferal to another ship to take command. There was, however, something slightly unusual about who was taking his place.

Adnah Caldin's fresh start wasn't going very smoothly. He had actually been the skipper of the *Owl* for just three months when he was transferred to the *Partridge* to take command from Snipes. It was an oddly short period of time that didn't escape notice. Officers and crew alike speculated: Was there an incident that led to the transferal? Was there a larger personality clash that couldn't be resolved?

There is no concrete answer; only clues. For example, on June 1, 1943, a crew member Fireman 1st Class W.E. Boydte returned to the *Owl* "dirty and disorderly." He was placed, by order of Lt. Caldin, in irons, a highly unusual punishment in the modern Navy, even in 1943. The punishment is so unusual that it is difficult to find reference to irons and the Navy not dated in the 19th century. It was the kind of novel punishment Caldin was fond of.

His transfer to the *Partridge* after such a short period of time may have been the Navy's way of heading off what it perceived as a personality conflict aboard a ship. The *Partridge* became Caldin's second chance at command. And Caldin, unlike White, was a career Navy man. Like many serving in the military between the wars, advancement was difficult and a career was seldom a straight and certain path.

Caldin joined the Navy as a 17-year-old. He saw combat in WWI off the coast of France, battling submarines aboard the *Christabel* and was aboard the *Osprey* on her maiden voyage to clear the Great Barrage. After serving on merchant vessels between 1922 and 1924, he rejoined the Navy as a seaman, attending submarine school and eventually serving aboard the *S-45*. In 1933, Caldin "made rate"—meaning that he was promoted to Petty Officer 3rd Class and given a job specialty. For Caldin this was Boatswain's Mate 3rd Class. From there on out, his career advanced at a remarkable rate. From 1933-39 he moved up the ratings from Boatswain's Mate 3rd Class to 2nd Class to 1st Class and finally onto Chief Boatswain, at the time the highest enlisted rank achievable. Appointed Boatswain in October of 1933, he was attached to the USS *Teal* and *Gannet*—both Lapwing minesweeper Bird Boats.

Caldin's rise in rank was swift and promising. But then it stalled.

During the fitting out of the USS *Lexington* in November of 1942, only a few months after this appointment, he requested that his temporary appointment of lieutenant be made permanent. The request was denied. The promotions stopped.

The Navy may not have seen fit to promote Adnah Caldin but, given his record, he was a clear choice to skipper a ship like the *Partridge* in wartime. He possessed experience in combat and had served as a senior officer aboard three Bird Boats before relieving Snipes of command. Compared to Jim White, Caldin's record shows a confident, capable, and experienced leader with a proven record. Moreover, he was a man who would continue to serve his country long after the war was over. Jim White would obtain a civilian job (he eventually became an optometrist) while Caldin would continue in the Navy for a decade or more.

The Navy was making a safe bet. A few bumps in an initial command were an inconvenience easily remedied by simply swapping commands. White's over-familiarity with the *Partridge* crew and Caldin's personality conflicts aboard the *Owl* were separate problems with a mutual solution.

In early December of 1943, Joe Cooney sat down and started another letter to Florie.

> *"I don't know the score yet, but I'm hoping to get one more weekend before we leave here. If everything goes right I may be home Saturday. I hope. I've been laid up the last week with a nasty cold. Just getting over it but it sure had me down. My room is being tore apart again; another new officer just came on board, that makes seven of us now; he and I share the same room after they put another bunk in."*

That other officer was a young ensign fresh out of college named Mike Rich. Stepping down into the beat up little boat was like stepping into another, wholly unexpected world.

Rich had grown up during the Depression in Latrobe, Pennsylvania. His father had served during WWI as a sergeant and was a business school graduate. His mother was a nurse. He lived with his twin sister and parents, and although life wasn't luxurious, the family was better off than most in those tough years.

After Pearl Harbor, Rich's options in life changed. As a college student, he was given the choice of completing his degree among several military track programs. He opted to work toward a Navy commission.

College programs kicked into high gear. Gone were the leisurely breaks in the summer, replaced instead by 12-month class schedules. He graduated from St. Vincent in January 1943 and received notice of his commission in February. With no fanfare, Rich and his father traveled to a train station near Latrobe and he reported to active duty at Fort Schuyler, New York. After officer training and completing his submarine attack training, Rich reported for duty aboard the *Partridge*.

This was Rich's through-the-looking-glass moment. Theories and standard operating procedures were thrown out the window. What he was entering into was a world suddenly set into turmoil. After four years of cruising the Caribbean, the ship was being overhauled in dry-dock in Norfolk. New equipment was being added and the small ship being made smaller to accommodate additional crew and officers. The officers alone would nearly double in size from five up to nine by the time the ship set sail for Europe. For Rich, the cramped quarters, the noise, and the decaying conditions of the ship were as far from Latrobe and college as he could imagine.

Entering his cabin for the first time, Rich was confronted by a burly Irishman who had spent a lifetime on the docks and harbors of New York City, a veteran of WWI and a father of four. Their close quarters aboard the *Partridge* ensured they would either be at each other's throats or become quick friends. Whether through luck or necessity, the latter happened.

Joe Cooney and Frank Lefavor in Bermuda, 1943

At first, Cooney cast a wary eye on his new bunkmate for his inexperience and naivety, but broke the ice by mocking the young officer for bringing aboard a small washboard to scrub his socks.

Cooney and Rich were a perfect example of the wide range of backgrounds and experience brought together by America to fight WWII. Rich, a middle-class college graduate from a landlocked portion of Pennsylvania, was soon fast friends with Cooney, a tugboat captain from Staten Island, full of tales about the characters that populated the docks of New York between the wars.

In fact, many of the friendships that evolved during the tour of the Caribbean were cemented during the November leave as the ship was being refurbished. My grandfather, Thurman Krouse, lived a relatively short bus ride from Norfolk and brought five of his shipmates home on the leave—an event that was big news in

Chewsville, Maryland, particularly in an era of small-town newspapers.

MRS. KROUSE IS GIVEN A SURPRISE

Husband Calls Wife at Chewsville After Duty in Trinidad

Imagine the surprise of Mrs. Thurman K. Krouse, of Chewsville when her husband telephoned here Tuesday evening stating he was in Hagerstown with five of his buddies. The young men have just returned from duty in Trinidad BWI and were granted a few hours. Since Mr. Krouse was the only one of the six close to home he invited them to visit his home.

An impromptu party was immediately arranged by Mrs. Krouse in honor of the young men and a delightful evening was spent listening to the tales the young sailors told, playing games, singing, and playing records.

The men were well pleased with the new life they are leading, and are very enthusiastic about their work. They have a nice coat of tan from being in the tropics and have all gained weight since enlisting. They said the meals they get are as good as the ones they used to get at home and as a whole, they are proud to be serving their country in the U.S. Navy.

Mike Donavan, Don Wampler, and Doris and Thurman Krouse
before the Partridge sailed to Europe

This upbeat story could not have been better written as a piece of propaganda by the war office. In fact, it was probably written by my grandmother, impeccably recorded on the Royal KMM typewriter she had used during her employment at Fairchild Aircraft. To readers, it was probably comforting, if not misleading about conditions in other theaters of war.

Some men took these final leaves to tie up loose ends. John Scherer, who had helped create the Donald Duck banner for the ship, had spoken with Bill Ames about getting married to his girl back in New York City. When the opportunity presented itself, he did just that.

Bill Ames made a long bus ride back to the Midwest to see his sweetheart Dotty before shipping out. Joe Feeney took the time to visit his family in South Boston. While there he paid a call to a young woman he knew from the neighborhood, Betty Hayes. He would write to her of his journey home—parts of the country were as foreign to him as anywhere in the Caribbean and Europe:

"The train stopped at a railroad junction in Pennsylvania; I looked through the window with that 'out of this world' stare I acquired, since dating you."

"I thought I saw three nuns, with three Jewish Rabbis!! I rubbed my eyes, but upon closer inspection, I noticed they were those 'Pennsylvania Dutch' people known as the 'Amish'."

"I'm sure you read about them. Perchance you haven't they are 'tillers of the soil,' and have no affiliation whatsoever with the United States Government."

"The husbands had beards that hung over their chests (Boy! Was I 'green with envy.')"

"Their wives looked exactly like the nuns up at Saint Brigid's, even so far as to having that stern look on their face too!"

Feeney's letters maintain a cheerful, consistently upbeat, 'aw shucks' tone that reminds us that shipping off to war was not only a solemn duty, but also a great adventure.

"Betty, remember the last night, we were together, and you wanted to know what I was laughing at? Well, believe it or not, it was that look on your face, when I took off my glove, to shake your hand. Honestly. I think if I socked you on the jaw, that hurt look on your face wouldn't have been half so

bad. Not that I'm bragging, or anything to that effect, but I'll never, in a lifetime, forget it."

Joe was part of a close-knit part of the crew all from New England—Rich Melanson, Angelo Mendello, Joe Mendello (both from New Haven, no relation), Stanley Menard, Joe Meskell, Paul Walton, and Tom Buffum, a young Quaker lieutenant recently graduated from Brown University.

Another member of the crew from New England was Joe Shannon. Shannon grew up in South Boston and had a shot at a baseball career with the Boston Braves. But they told him he was too young and he should finish high school. After the war broke out, Shannon and his brother joined the Navy. His brother was assigned to the USS *Washington*, and Shannon to the *Partridge*. Although he joined late and missed most of the ship's adventures in the Caribbean, Shannon would become one of the most reliable sources of information about the ship's last days in the war.

These were uncertain times for the *Partridge*. The men that had served in the Caribbean experienced the dark days early in the war when the little ship seemed to be the only thing standing in the way of U-boat domination on the East Coast.

But two years later, the sub threat had all but been eradicated. Carriers and long-range bomber support meant that in 1943, for the first time, German U-boats no longer had safe havens in the Atlantic. These tactics took their toll on men like Albrecht Achilles, commander of the *U-161*. He was killed on September 27, 1943, along with his entire crew, when the sub was destroyed by depth charges dropped from a U.S. Mariner aircraft off the coast of Bahia. He was one of the hundreds of U-boat crew members lost in the Atlantic as Germany's initially exuberant success turned into a pointless sacrifice. Suffering heavy losses, Admiral Dönitz called off his attacks on Allied convoys, ending one of the longest and most damaging submarine campaigns in history. For the U-boats, the Happy Time was over.

Al and Dotty Riker during leave in Norfolk

For the *Partridge,* there seemed to be light at the end of the tunnel. The duty schedule that had been so hectic at the outset eased up. No longer was the *Partridge* called upon to rescue crews dumped into the water—instead, towing duty took priority. Occasionally towing a target sled for destroyers to practice on was the cause for excitement (and the occasional near-miss). But, generally, the ship had occupied a slow, uneventful backwater on the periphery of the war.

Now there was a new captain and a new mission in a new place somewhere far across the Atlantic. As the crew convened aboard the ship and she left dry dock, the *Partridge* was far from "like-new." But she was improved. She had an increased retinue of officers, new radar equipment, new paint, a clean deck, and newer navigational aids. Most important, she had a new lease on life. The Caribbean wouldn't be her last cruise. Now there were rumors of a mission in Europe or Africa. Rumors that peppered conversations and letters home in homemade codes along with Christmas and New Year's wishes. But winter storms were gathering in the Atlantic, and many looked to sea nervously. Some were facing life on the open ocean for the first time, and many of the more experienced crew, with memories of warm tropical water, were looking at the violent Atlantic in winter as the true enemy.

All the anxiety gathering in November and December was punctuated by one question: who was the new captain? Aside from rumors and hearsay, little was known about who would replace Captain Snipes. On December 14, 1944, Lt. Adnah Caldin stepped aboard. Less than 24 hours later, the ship departed across the Atlantic as part of Task Force 66.

Caldin was stepping into a challenging situation. The men aboard were a close-knit family with a long history of service in a different theater of combat. It was a situation that could work both for and against a ship's captain. The collective power of a crew, in the end, supersedes any direct power of a captain. In addition, Caldin was taking the ship into an entirely different war. For all the sub-dodging, chasing, and salvage conducted in the Caribbean, the colder waters of the North Atlantic and the crowded English Channel would require new skills, and new styles of leadership.

But for an experienced career naval officer, these challenges should not have been insurmountable. In fact, they were not unusual circumstances. His approach to these challenges would make all the difference.

There were several traits about Caldin that men noted almost immediately. First, he adhered to a more formal command structure than previous captains. Caldin wanted to run a tight ship and he expected his officers to be an extension of this credo. It was an obvious change from the styles of Snipes or Kenney and not an entirely strange or even inappropriate style of command, given the new situation.

But Caldin began his command aboard the Partridge with a blunder that even a young ensign just out of school recognized as strange.

"He didn't dine with other officers, which I thought was strange," Mike Rich recalled some 65 years later.

It was strange. A picture of Caldin aboard the USS *Gannett* shows him dining cordially with other officers. Even on a larger vessel, where there is greater space both physically and socially between ranks, a captain dining with his officers offers an opportunity to exchange news of the day, share ideas on running the ship, and, in general, build a strong working bond. Even as the *Partridge* was just beginning its long voyage across the wintry Atlantic, her command was already in question.

The end of 1943 was a watershed moment not just for the *Partridge* but for the war in general. For the U.S. and its allies, it was a time for optimism. In the past year, the Soviets had liberated Leningrad and Kiev and saw a massive surrender of encircled German forces at Stalingrad. Allies had pushed Germany out of North

Africa, landed in Sicily and Italy, and were pushing up the peninsula, eventually receiving the surrender of Italy and that country's declaration of war on Germany. In the Pacific, the Americans were inflicting heavy blows against the Japanese. Admiral Yamamoto, Japan's combined fleet commander and the architect of the attack on Pearl Harbor, was killed when his plane was shot down by American P-38s. U.S. Marines landed on Bougainville and Tarawa, pushing back further to the Japanese homeland.

Adnah Caldin (second officer seated from the right) with other officers aboard the USS Gannett prior to commanding the Partridge

It was the year that Americans and the Allies began to see hope. The seemingly invincible German and Japanese war machine was finally beginning to crumble.

For the *Partridge,* 1943 marked the end of its service close to home. Gone were the weekend home visits. The surprise brief appearances. Now the ship was sailing to a far-off place an ocean away. It was the beginning of a new and defining chapter in the history of the *Partridge*; her war service would no longer be about ad hoc operations to salvage whatever could be saved and staunch the wounds inflicted by U-boat attacks. Now, they were taking the fight directly to the enemy.

Most sailors aboard the *Partridge* and the hundreds of other vessels sailing for the U.K. didn't yet know it, but they would participate in one of the most historic operations at sea—a great conflict waged off the coast of Normandy. For Adnah Caldin, Jim White, Mike Rich, Joe Cooney, Bill Ames, and others aboard the ship, it would also be a time of great conflict waged on board their own ship.

An unknown sailor, Joe Mendello, Joe Meskell, and Angie Mendello probably in Norfolk before shipping out for Europe.

Chapter 6
Crossing Over

Irving Yaffe clung tightly to the rail of the ship as bitter December winds bit at his face. Like many young men who signed up to serve their country, Yaffe had quickly found himself in a completely foreign and utterly hostile environment.

The Northern Atlantic in winter is a notoriously rough and unpredictable environment: a brutal tempest of frigid water, wind, snow, and ice. Even aboard large freighters, warships, and cruise liners, the high winds and rough seas of the Atlantic in winter have, at their least, caused great discomfort for passengers, and at their worst, have damaged and sunk ships. Large, modern ships have been struck and even lost by encounters with rogue waves up to 100 feet high. The *Partridge* could easily be sent to the bottom by a wave a fraction of that size.

For Yaffe, a young kid from Brooklyn, the seas buffeting the diminutive *Partridge* must have seemed like the end of the world. And as wave after wave washed over the deck, the watch turned into a desperate struggle against nature just to remain on board.

Through sheets of rain, Yaffe spotted a place of refuge. The one spot on deck that he could safely fulfill his watch duties but remain somewhat protected from the elements: the portside fireroom ventilator. It may have been a refuge of Yaffe's own making or one that had served other crew members well in rainy weather. Perhaps it was a well-known trick that had served many a cold, wet sailor well in calmer waters. But in seeking shelter on that stormy December night, Yaffe sealed his fate as the first man to die on the ship during WWII.

The weather that drove Yaffe into the ventilation shaft was, for many men aboard the ship, the first taste of what the open sea in foul weather could be.

In a way, Irving Yaffe's search for safety reflected how the entire crew clung to their ship for comfort. It is what sailors do to keep journeys upon the open ocean tolerable. A ship is their home and entire world, no matter how small. And in a small world like the *Partridge* being tossed about in the tumult of the wintery North Atlantic crossing, there can be a creeping sense that the entire world is about to come to a violent end.

The frigid waters were especially terrifying given what lurked beneath: a gauntlet of submarines that sent thousands of ships to the bottom of the Atlantic. A submarine attack and the frigid waters were the dominant thoughts of anyone aboard a surface vessel in these waters at the time.

The war in the Atlantic had not started well for Germany. Submarines were penned in by the shallow and well-mined English Channel, and torpedo technology failed more often than not. However, as tactics changed, losses became devastating. Admiral Dönitz's "wolf packs" would spread out along convoy lines and, when they spotted a target, would zero in and attack en masse. Often military escorts would break off in pursuit of a single sub, leaving others free to attack unarmed merchant vessels.

The Allies were turning the tide through new technology and tactics of the own. In the end, it was sheer production numbers that won over: they were able to produce more tonnage than the German U-boat fleet could send to the bottom of the Atlantic. After 1943, losses to the Allies would fall off precipitously. But there was no way of knowing that in December of 1943. At that point in the war over 2,000 ships had been lost along with over 21,000 merchant sailors; most died in the water minutes after a submarine strike forced them off ships. It became known as the Battle of the Atlantic.

What sent Irving Yaffe into the icy North Atlantic was not a German torpedo—it was a large wave washing over the deck of the *Partridge* that ripped the ventilator off the deck and plunged it into the icy water. Yaffe went with it. The deck crew saw what happened and immediately alerted the bridge. The signal went out to the convoy and the *Partridge* peeled off using its searchlights to cut through the curtains of rain and sea spray that engulfed the night. Amid the white caps of 20-foot waves, it would have been a minor miracle to find the waving arms of Yaffe. More than likely, the waving arms of the young "Jewish fella from Brooklyn" were trapped in the heavy metal tube of the ventilator well on their way to the bottom of the ocean.

Most men aboard the *Partridge* had little experience with convoys and the tumultuous North Atlantic was a completely new landscape. But one man had the experience of both war and the dangers of the sea that would be invaluable in guiding the ship across the Atlantic and through any adversity that lie ahead.

Adnah Caldin was a veteran of WWI and of the Bird Boats in general. As a young man, Caldin had sailed on the USS *Auk,* which was caught up in a violent storm and nearly lost off Long Island. It was just one of a series of points along Caldin's career that seemed to make him an ideal leader for the ship's new role in the European theater.

Caldin had joined the Navy as a patriotic duty when the U.S. entered WWI in 1918. He had witnessed action off of France aboard the civilian yacht turned patrol craft USS *Cristabel*.

Like many young boys, Caldin entered the Navy to serve his country seeking the danger and adventure that a war offers. For some, abrupt violence ends all delusions. For most, the tedious rituals of military life quickly overshadow dreams of glory. Caldin's experience was the rare exception. He found an immediate role model in a young ensign named Daniel Sullivan.

Sullivan enrolled in the U.S. Naval Reserves and was then commissioned as an ensign. On the *Chistabel*, he encountered his first combat at sea. Without hesitation the ensign dashed toward a number of unsecured depth charges loose on the deck of the *Christabel*, throwing himself against them, securing them to the side of the ship, and saving the ship and her crew from almost certain destruction. His actions earned him the Medal of Honor.

The taste of combat and Sullivan's heroic actions impressed Caldin, whose experiences were limited to life in a saloon his father owned in Tidioute, Pennsylvania.

With a crew of only 66 on the *Christabel*, the young Caldin would have had daily contact with Sullivan. He was the model of everything that Caldin wanted throughout his entire naval career. While many people go to war and witness terrible scenes of carnage that obliterate their dreams of glory, others witness selfless acts of heroism that reinforce their own vision of how war can transform their own lives.

Sullivan's charge forward to secure the depth charges changed the trajectory of his life. And it was this change that Caldin was so desperate to achieve.

But, if Sullivan's acts were selfless, they were still attached to his status as a Navy officer. As much as Caldin's life in the Navy represented an escape from the life of a saloon owner's son, it was hardly an escape from the rigid class system of the U.S. Navy.

Chances to hunt submarines, disarm depth charges, and transcend life at home would soon be over. As the Great War wound to an end, Caldin saw little opportunity in the Navy for true advancement. Without a high school degree, he would forever be stuck below deck with little, if any, hope of obtaining the status of officer.

Sullivan would have a long and fruitful career in the Navy. He was eventually awarded the rank of lieutenant commander and received a plum assignment working in the Navy office in London after WWI was over.

Caldin, on the other hand, quit the Navy to complete his high school diploma only to return to the Navy in the early 1930s. After an initial burst of advancement in rank, a glacial career advancement took hold across the sleepy peacetime. After Pearl Harbor, Caldin's chances for career advancement dramatically increased. The Navy desperately needed officers with his experience and skill set. As the junior officer ranks filled with younger "90-day wonders," Caldin stood out as the vanguard career Navy officer. A promotion to lieutenant and command of his own vessel was not so much a high point for Caldin, but an opportunity for advancement that would make up for the decade spent in the lower ranks of a peacetime Navy.

Crossing the North Atlantic was the first great challenge of his wartime command. What lay ahead was a mystery, but it was clear that the ship was headed toward the nexus of the war in Europe. The heroic Sullivan moments were only possible in a wartime combat situation, and it was this test that Caldin felt was ahead of him. He was commanding a ship at sea during war and both the burden of command and its glory were in his hands.

But the *Partridge* was essentially a workship; an almost comically old vessel that lived up to its befuddled Donald Duck mascot. Her previous commanders seemed to understand the nature of command aboard a vessel her size and age and took those limitations in stride. They were captains of a U.S. Navy vessel, but they were also a father figure, a small town mayor, and a building super. Caldin saw his role and his ship, in a different light.

If Adnah Caldin had delusions about the grandeur of his command, the *Partridge* began to assert itself likewise. Shortly after leaving port on December 15, the rudder jammed in the bridge steering station. On December 17, the gyrocompass failed and the ship switched to the standard compass, making it more difficult to navigate the rough seas. Bill Ames, the sole crew member to know celestial navigation, provided guidance during the rest of the trip over. It was a skill that he would later find gave him enviable power aboard the ship.

The bad luck encountered by the *Partridge* during the first days of her crossing could be racked up to just that: bad luck. The loss of a crew member was a tragedy but a reality of life at sea. As for the mechanical and equipment failures, they were moderate challenges to be expected on a ship the *Partridge's* age. No single event occurred during the crossing that adversely affected the disposition of a crew nor the ability of a captain to command. Yet it is during these events that Caldin began to display what many would describe as strange behavior.

At first, officers noticed he was avoiding almost all casual contact with them. Mike Rich's observation of Caldin not dining with the other officers seemed both odd and counterproductive, particularly during the crossing when he was getting to know the ship and its crew. Officers who had far more experience aboard the ship would have been invaluable to a new captain, essentially thrown into the command of a ship only hours before it departed on a long sea voyage.

But as the journey continued, Caldin's command style emerged more distinctly. He demanded a "battle plan" from Mike Rich who, even as a young ensign, recognized that it was a ridiculous request.

"We were a workship that didn't need a battle plan. You just didn't waste your time with stuff like that. It was just ridiculous."

Caldin began issuing more orders that simply didn't make sense. During the crossing, one such written order outlined that traditional telescopic spyglasses were to be used instead of standard issue binoculars. Long glasses had not been used in the Navy for decades and it is difficult to determine why a captain would order a crew to use them when binoculars were more effective in terms of depth perception and ease of use. The order was inefficient and ripe for parody—indeed, sailors literally laughed at the devices supplied by Caldin, wondering if he picked them up at a dime-store in Norfolk. But the joke wore thin as they struggled to steady them even in moderately rough weather.

Not only was the order ludicrous—it was executed in a way that ultimately weakened Caldin's authority. Officers were given no reason for the request—the captain's authority was absolute and the order stood, but it was power squandered on a petty, meaningless gesture.

And yet Caldin was steadfast in enforcing the order with the crew. Signalman 1st Class Sam Aldebet was to be the first example of what would happen if an order, petty or not, were disobeyed. According to Bill Ames, Aldebet was a good sailor who had a few problems here or there but basically performed well.

Aldebet was struggling to comply with the order, but using a spyglass in rough seas proved too difficult and he switched to binoculars. He found himself brought before a captain's mast.

A captain's mast is not a trial. It is classified in Article 15 of the Uniform Code of Military Justice as a Commanding Officer's non-judicial punishment. In the article, there is a list of circumstances and punishments that can be administered and a reduction of rank is listed. Caldin announced the verdict and punishment: Aldebet was guilty and would receive a reduction in rank and pay for disobeying the orders of a senior officer.

Caldin was within his rights, but the punishment was grossly disproportionate to the crime. To the officers and the crew, the incident seemed like a foolish waste of time that undermined their ability to accomplish their ship's mission.

Bill Ames had taken on the duties of chief master at arms—it was his job to enforce both official Navy regulations and the rules of the ship that the captain adhered to. Ames was present at Aldebet's mast and the many others that followed. (Mike Rich recalled a captain's mast every Friday, though the ship's log shows they sometimes occurred two or three times in a week.) At the end of the hearing, Caldin turned to Ames wagging an accusatory finger. "You're next..."

It was a threat that Ames took seriously. As opposed to the cordial relationship Ames had with previous captains, an especially rocky one had developed with Caldin. It had started with the mechanical difficulties that the *Partridge* faced at sea. When the rudder became stuck during the crossing, Ames found himself running afoul of the Captain's capricious temper. Unjamming the rudder required going below deck and manipulating the steering drum that could easily crush a hand if it was in motion during the repair. Ames warned the deck crew of what he was doing and was adamant that no one was to touch the ship's wheel.

Ames descended below deck into the cramped chamber that housed the drum. He placed his hands onto the drum to loosen the chain connecting it to the rudder. Suddenly he felt his fingers being pulled inside as the drum began to move. Pulling back just in time, Ames could see someone was manipulating the wheel on the bridge. He grabbed the com and berated the person on the bridge with a string of obscenities common aboard many Navy ships—but the question was clear: Who was on the bridge and why were they messing with the wheel during the repair?

A silence greeted Ames' request. Then a response from the Captain.

"Ames, report to the bridge immediately."

Caldin wasted no time laying in to Ames for his behavior, reminding him that addressing a senior officer was a strict violation of Navy codes. Further, this was his ship and he would do anything he damned well please on the bridge (no matter that such actions could have easily removed Ames' fingers).

But Ames knew better than to point out these contradictions. Taking verbal abuse was easier than the alternative. Yet Ames knew the end result: a reduction in rank. But he had worked too hard to rise from enlisted sailor to the rank of his chief quartermaster, the youngest sailor to do so up to that point in the U.S. Navy. He braced himself and interrupted the Captain gently reminding him that he was the only one aboard who knew the celestial navigation needed to complete the journey. A reduction in rank would bar him from the bridge and prevent these skills from being utilized. Ames wasn't even sure if that was true and held his breath. Caldin quietly dismissed him back to duty. There was no punishment and the ship navigated safely across the Atlantic reaching Horta Bay in the Azores on December 27, 1943.

The *Partridge* was steaming in a convoy of other newer minesweepers. These ships, unceremoniously numbered rather than named: YMS 348 – 352, steamed along retracing the journey of the Bird Boats almost 25 years earlier. By all accounts, the winter weather in the North Atlantic was rough and felt particularly acute in the small ships built for operations closer to shore. When the ships did reach their waypoint in the Azores 12 days after leaving port, the men were understandably eager for shore leave.

The Azores, the tip of the largest mountains in the world, rise out of the Atlantic in dramatic peaks reaching as high at 7,713 feet above sea level. Nine major and eight smaller islands make up the archipelago. They are a remote place: equidistant between Portugal and Newfoundland, but ruled by Portugal, which had fortified the islands with an expeditionary force to defend the country's neutrality from both Axis and Allies alike. However, the Portuguese government eventually allowed Allied bases to be established there in late 1943 in exchange for, among other things, a promise by the Allies to liberate East Timor, which had been taken by the Japanese in the Pacific.

For most of the sailors, the introduction to the Azores was their first truly exotic port of call. Cognac was the main drink available on the island and proved to be a potent release from life at sea.

In the Azores, the drunken conduct of sailors on shore was quickly the subject of a captain's mast. Swabbing the decks, confinement to the ship, and a restriction on further shore leaves was imposed. By this time, Lt. Caldin's captain's masts had become a regular event. There is one official infraction entered into the logs upon arrival in the Azores, when sailors Weber and Kozminzki arrived absent over leave and saw a reduction in rank. The punishments were unusually harsh for the infractions, particularly confining so many of the crew to the ship after such a long voyage.

The grumblings of the sailors who had their much-anticipated leave taken away was of less consequence to the captain than to the officers who commanded the men. Although the captain had complete authority over the ship, many of the officers had come to know these men and thought the punishment unfair.

Caldin, however, escalated the situation and restricted everyone to the ship for the duration of the convoy's stay in the Azores from December 29 until January 1, 1944. It would take another five days at sea to reach the ship's destination in Falmouth, England.

By this time, Caldin had solidified his reputation with the crew as a hard-nosed, unforgiving, dictatorial captain. Life under his command was not going to be easy and a small infraction by a sailor would cost the crew dearly in terms of precious leave from the ship or, perhaps worse, a reduction in rank and pay.

Yet Caldin's command style still was within the norm. Trouble with drunken disorderly sailors is common enough to have become a cliché. Lt. White experienced this firsthand during his crossing and subsequent stopover in the Azores while he commanded the *Owl*. Approximately two weeks behind the *Partridge*, the *Owl* pulled into the same port. Like Caldin, this was White's first command of sailors in a foreign port. But White faced an even greater challenge when one of his crew was accused of murder.

Of the two crossings, White's by far had a greater potential for conflict among the ranks. He faced a very real crisis during war-time, while Adnah Caldin dealt with some minor incidents during a rough crossing and the ship's first port-of-call.

But both ships were heading into a larger challenge yet. In England, the Allies were preparing for a massive invasion and part of it was an experimental plan to build an artificial harbor off the coast of Normandy: Operation Mulberry.

In the darkness of a cold December night in the middle of the North Atlantic, the *Partridge* swung out of formation with the convoy she was steaming with. It was 20:20 and high winds and rough seas had knocked out the portside ventilator, sweeping Seaman First Class Irving Herman Yaffe overboard.

A lighted buoy was released into the frigid water and a spotlight shone out over the peaked waves. After two hours of searching, they gave up and returned to the convoy. Joe Cooney wrote home to Florie saying:

> *"I hope you had a good Christmas. We had ours at sea and it was rough as hell all the whole trip. We lost a boy from Brooklyn on the way. He fell over the side at night."*

Joe Feeney wrote to Betty Hayes about the incident, noting of Jaffe:

> *"He was a Jewish fellow from Brooklyn and one of the swellest fellows I've ever met."*

Almost certainly, Yaffe plunged deep into the Atlantic along with the heavy metal object. If he did manage to make it to the surface, finding him in the storm would have been nearly impossible. He would succumb to hypothermia in a matter of minutes.

It was a time of war and hundreds of thousands of lives lost all over the world. However, for the men of *Partridge,* this was the first of the crew members to be lost since the beginning of the war. His death marked the moment that the *Partridge* crossed over into a new, and final, chapter in her history. They had entered waters more dangerous than any of them had ever encountered. And during this new and crucial stage they had no confidence in the man who held their fate in his hands.

Chapter 7
Captain Bligh Stories

In 1935, audiences across a Depression-weary nation were treated to a true Hollywood adventure classic. The film pits a vindictive and cruel captain against a freedom-seeking band of sailors led by Fletcher Christian. Charles Laughton stars as Captain Bligh and Clark Gable as Fletcher Christian. *Mutiny on the Bounty* embodies boyhood dreams of adventure on the high seas. With exotic locales, beautiful native women, daring adventure, and personal heroism, the film gave audiences what many still seek today in a movie: pure, uncomplicated melodrama.

Andre Sennwald reviewed the film in the *New York Times* on November 9, 1935:

> *"Grim, brutal, sturdily romantic, made out of horror and desperate courage, it is as savagely exciting and rousingly dramatic a photoplay as has come out of Hollywood in recent years."*

The film was, by any measure, immensely successful. It was the top-grossing film of 1935, bringing in over $4 million. It won an Oscar for best picture that year. *Bounty* was so pervasive in culture that the conflict between Bligh and Fletcher Christian was even depicted by Bugs Bunny and Yosemite Sam a decade after the film was released. The film took the cutlasses, muskets and tall masts of backyard play and crystallized them in a thrilling true-life saga of good versus evil. It was Charles Laughton's superb portrayal of a perverse and cruel Bligh that stole the show.

Sennwald's review praised Laughton's performance as Bligh calling it:

> "...a fascinating and almost unbearable portrait of a sadist who took rapturous delight in watching men in pain. We get the full horror of his personality early in the film when a seaman, convicted of striking an officer, is ordered to be lashed on every vessel in the fleet. Brought to the Bounty, he is discovered to be already dead from his previous floggings, but Bligh, observing the cold letter of the regulations, insists that the corpse receive the appointed forty lashes in full view of his officers and men. His penalties for minor offenses are the judgments of a maniac. From the swish of the lash, he derives a lewd joy."

Laughton's performance isn't the top-hatted mustachioed villain of the silent era. His Bligh is made for the Hollywood close-up capturing every bead of nervous sweat and facial tick.

Bligh here is an insane maniac. Not just a harsh disciplinarian who believes that strict authority brings about better performance, but a person who actually takes perverse pleasure in the pain of others. Laughton's characterization goes even further than the lashings decried in the review. His Bligh eventually keel-hauls a sailor for complaining about lack of water.

Keel-hauling did exist in the navies and merchant ships at the time, but it was rarely used because it often resulted in death. In it a man would be dragged under the hull of a ship from one side to the other, scraping against the barnacle-encrusted ship and emerging on the other side, more than likely, drowned or bleeding to death.

Laughton's powerful performance defined Bligh for generations of movie-goers. And for many teenage boys in 1935, the film defined the nature of naval authority. They would use "Bligh" as an outsized, cartoonish comparison—the equivalent of referring to an overzealous store clerk or office manager as a Nazi. It was no doubt Laughton's Bligh that many a seaman saw in officers imposing the harsh realities of military life on them during the war.

The realities were far more complex. Herman Wouk cautioned against comparisons between the modern Navy and the world of tall ships and cannons in his introduction to *Caine:*

> *"It was not a mutiny in the old-time sense, of course, with flashing of cutlasses, a captain in chains, and desperate sailors turning outlaws. After all, it happened in 1944 in the United States Navy."*

There were no lashes, no keel hauling, no sadistic grins or lewd joy in the modern Navy. But, in fact, Wouk's statement about 1944 and the United States Navy is less applicable. It would be more fitting to point out that the flashing cutlasses, evil captains, and simplified storylines were never very true to begin with. They were more a Hollywood fiction than history.

What actually happened aboard the *Bounty* shows how a breakdown of a ship's command structure is possible. The complexity of command, mission, crew, and plain human interaction cannot be written off as solely the result of an abjectly cruel personality. At least not in the case of the *Bounty*. Queeg and Caldin were not Captain Bligh. Nor was Captain Bligh.

The details of the *Bounty's* mission were mundane and commercial. But this trading mission has become one of the most definitive stories of the sea and has largely influenced our ideas of ship life in everything from modern novels about the sail era to *Star Trek*.

When she sailed from England in 1787, the *Bounty* was on an expedition to the South Seas to acquire breadfruit meant to feed slaves in the West Indies. Lieutenant Bligh commanded the relatively small cutter. In the winter of 1787 – 88, Bligh attempted to access the South Pacific around Cape Horn, which would have significantly cut short the journey. After a full month of trying, Bligh turned the ship around and sailed across the less tumultuous Cape of Good Hope, reaching Tahiti on October 26, 1788. On the journey, Bligh demoted John Fryer, the ship's sailing master. He promoted a young man to the position, naming him acting lieutenant, Fletcher Christian.

After spending five months in Tahiti, the ship set sail for the Caribbean on April 4, 1789. Despite various accounts including in several films, Bligh did not once again try to round Cape Horn helping to spark the mutiny. Nevertheless, mutiny did break out on April 28, 1789, resulting in Bligh being set adrift with 18 men who remained loyal (a total of 22 remained loyal but four stayed with the Bounty due to lack of room) in a 23-foot launch heavily loaded and equipped only with a sextant and a pocket watch. The launch was so overloaded that its sides were only a few inches above the water. In open seas, the journey was tantamount to a death sentence.

Bligh navigated the tiny craft to Tofua, where they encountered hostile natives who killed one of his crew. Bligh then turned the craft to the closest European outpost, Timor, which was located an incredible 3,618 nautical miles away. After 47 days, the tiny boat reached the outpost with no further casualties.

Bligh's actual unraveling of command seems remarkably short on details. Least accurate but most persistent is the image of a cruel, borderline-insane leader hell-bent on accomplishing a mission with little regard for the health and safety of his men. Another view is of a clash of personalities between Christian and Bligh, which appeals to our relationship-based view of leadership and management today. Both theories probably grew out of the public relations and legal battles waged for decades after the incident and Bligh's misfortunes in command afterward.

Bligh returned to Britain from his storied open boat journey a hero. Throughout the trials of the mutineers (a number of whom were eventually captured and tried in England) Bligh's reputation remained intact. But Fletcher Christian's family waged an intense publicity campaign deriding Bligh's capability as a leader and contributing to the idea that Christian may have been acting in the best interest of the men aboard the *Bounty*.

But an abjectly cruel Bligh just isn't supported by the facts.

Bligh's pathway to a complete loss of control over his ship was reflected a century later in Captain Queeg. Bligh's measuring of coconuts to prove that theft was taking place aboard the *Bounty* is widely credited with inspiring the strawberry incident in *Caine*—demonstrating a captain's obsession with detail and, perhaps, descent into madness. But the *Bounty*'s mutiny also shares other traits that seem more at home in the 20th century than in the cutlass-and-sail world of the 1840s.

The first cracks in Bligh's command happened in Tasmania. After failing to cross into the Pacific around the Horn of Africa, Bligh rounded the tip of South America and took on repairs in the island port off the Southern tip of Australia. During this stay-over, Bligh severely criticized the ship's carpenter for cutting billets of wood poorly. The carpenter, William Purcell, eventually became so enraged at Bligh's micromanaging that the captain was forced to order him back aboard the ship. Being short of hands, Bligh chose not to confine the man to quarters and flogging was not an option for Purcell's rank of chief warrant officer.

The stay in Tasmania was further troubled by the ship's first death on the journey. A young sailor was bled by the ship's surgeon for a routine treatment of an ailment. The sailor's wounds became infected and he eventually died. Bligh strongly criticized the ship's surgeon for the sailor's treatment and the rest of the officers for failing to recognize symptoms early enough.

In Tahiti, a major desertion incident was resolved swiftly and efficiently—the men were found, tried, and punished: Bligh was light on the men—letting them off with a flogging instead of deferring to a trial back home, which could have resulted in hanging. The men were, in fact, grateful to Bligh for his leniency.

The desertion was a threat to the *Bounty*'s mission. With a small crew, the loss of manpower would have put in jeopardy the return voyage home. But if Bligh showed restraint in his punishment of the deserters, he held his officers accountable for their behavior, starting with Midshipman Thomas Heyward who fell asleep when the desertion took place. Starting in January of 1889, Bligh began to compile a long list of complaints against his officers culminating in the infamous accusation of Fletcher Christian for the theft of coconuts.

We may never know the motivations of Fletcher Christian in leading a mutiny or those of the men who followed him. He may have simply acted out of anger and frustration without thinking through the consequences. Or he may have been inspired by glimpses of freedom from the titled life that waited for him at home. Needless to say, the ship's distance from government and law and order and its isolation on the far edges of the Earth, combined with Christian's motivations, the tension with other officers, and Bligh's temperament to create a perfect storm. A storm too complex to blame on one cause, but one that led to the loss of his command.

When Bligh returned home, he was court marshaled and found to be not at fault for the insurrection. There is little, if any, evidence that he subjected his crew to excessive punishment. In fact, Bligh often scolded crew members when many other captains would have chosen the whip.

In addition, the trial revealed Bligh to be an exceptionally capable seaman. His navigation skills, acquired under the direction of the venerable Captain Cook, were second to none. This proved useful during the open sea voyage but must also have been evident during his command of the *Bounty*.

His leadership during the 48-day open-boat voyage also suggests that Bligh was a capable leader.

While other islands lay within a more reasonable sailing distance, Bligh was steadfast in his decision to head for Timor, weighing the considerable risks of a longer voyage against the threat of hostile natives. There must have been significant doubt, spoken or unspoken, from the crew during the voyage, but Bligh held firm.

Bligh's skills at sea were beyond reproach and he proved again and again that he was a capable and even brilliant leader of men.

So what did happen? If the mutiny wasn't caused by an external, nefarious plot on the part of Fletcher Christian, and it wasn't caused by unreasonable tyranny or sheer incompetence, what was the cause?

It may have been that Bligh was less of a cruel taskmaster and more of a micromanager who alienated himself from those who could have made him a stronger leader. This was an unfortunate habit that conspired against him not just during the voyage of the *Bounty* but throughout his career.

"[Bligh made] dogmatic judgements which he felt himself entitled to make; he saw fools about him too easily... thin-skinned vanity was his curse through life... [Bligh] never learnt that you do not make friends of men by insulting them," wrote J.C. Beaglehole, biographer of Captain Cook. Bligh may simply have lacked empathy. And that made him, for lack of a better word, unlikable. Much like his command aboard the *Bounty*, his later career began to unravel and his personality did little to prevent or slow its demise.

After the *Bounty,* he was in command of ship during the *Spithead* mutiny as well as the mutiny at the Royal Navy anchorage of *Nore*, but there is no evidence that he was directly responsible. Both the *Spithead* mutinies and the *Nore* mutiny were widespread insurrections among British Navy ships whose crews demanded a better distribution of prize money and an end to cruelty. Be that as it may, it was during the *Nore* mutiny that Bligh learned of his nickname among sailors and officers of the fleet: "That Bounty Bastard."

Despite these setbacks, he went on to lead ships into battle under Nelson in the Battles of Copenhagen and Camperdown. In both cases, he was praised for his loyalty, courage, and seamanship. Bligh was rewarded for his actions with a plum appointment as Governor of New South Wales in March 1805. He arrived in August 1806 and less than a year and a half later, the Rum Rebellion erupted. Bligh was forced to sail from Sydney aboard the HMS *Porpoise,* where he remained effectively imprisoned until 1810, when relief finally arrived.

It appears that Bligh was not a cruel taskmaster or an extreme disciplinarian. In fact, he was chosen for commands based on his reputation for tough but fair leadership. At least on two occasions he acted in ways that eroded the support of his officers. This was, more than likely, the ultimate source of his undoing.

In the case of the *Bounty,* Bligh's promotion of Christian to essentially second in command over a longtime naval officer undermined his support among the officers. The more they questioned his decisions, the more he distanced himself from them. Bligh firmly believed that he, above all others, knew the correct way of running a ship, and often held his officers accountable for shortfalls in the crew. Although a captain answers to no one particularly when alone on the high seas, Bligh may have cared more about this singular fact while ignoring the storm clouds gathering around his command. Whether it was losing the support of his officers aboard the *Bounty* or the confidence of the militia men in Australia, Bligh was not inept at command so much as he was ignorant of the empathy necessary to be an effective leader.

Although Wouk goes out of his way to point out the differences between the *Caine* and *Bounty*, the conditions aboard the ships were remarkably similar. They were both relatively small ships with fewer than 75 sailors and officers aboard. Neither ship had a large officer class. Both were commanded by Lieutenants. Queeg and Bligh were both in their early thirties despite being depicted in film as being much older men.

The other common trait among these ships and captains was their isolation. The *Bounty* was far from home or any other Navy ships. Exposure to the Tahitian climate and natives for over four months may have meant that her crew simply could not readjust to strict life aboard a ship and were so isolated that the only world they could imagine anymore was in the blue waters around them.

During WWII the lure of island life was less of a draw (too much combat was taking place on land) but the *Caine* operates in highly independent ways, often performing duties that changed from day to day. The ship drew less attention from higher authorities and gave the crews and officers a sense that they alone controlled their fate under leaders whom they distrusted.

The Captain Bligh stories that Wouk referred to in his 1945 memo may have gained a chuckle or two in the offices of the Secretary of the Navy, but they were closer to the truth than Wouk or anyone else probably imagined. Wouk's reference to the historic figure more than likely evoked the cruel taskmaster of Laughton's portrayal.

But Bligh's downfall was not in being cruel; it was in being beyond reproach. And Wouk was reacting to the basic naval philosophy in his memo and his novel. If the captain is always right then a good deal of men from the reserves will be wrong. Their voices will never be heard and the Navy will be weaker for it.

A Navy memo dated May 4, 1944, from the Commander, Landing Craft and Bases, Eleventh Amphibious Force to the Chief of Naval Personnel, outlines conditions aboard a minesweeper serving in the English Channel preparing for D-Day. It could have been written about both the *Caine* and the *Bounty*:

> *"That such conditions should be allowed to exist on any ship of the U.S. Navy can only partially be condoned by 1.) The type of duty the ship has been doing which has been for the most part independent towing operations in this theatre with little or no opportunity for responsible seniors to observe the conditions on board, and 2.) The inexperience of the junior officers resulting in lack of knowledge as to how to inform the proper seniors at an earlier date..."*

But the memo was not written about the *Caine* or the *Bounty*. It was written about the USS *Partridge*. The Navy already knew the dangers of Captain Bligh stories a full year before Wouk wrote his memo. At least after the fact, the Navy was willing to recognize that a captain and officer within the Navy—even an officer of some record—could be incompetent.

As the *Partridge* sailed toward England, Caldin's leadership entered a dangerous new stage. His harsh treatment of enlisted men began to bring him directly into conflict with his officers. A world away from tall ships and "cutlasses and muskets," Caldin was committing the same fateful error as Bligh. Losing confidence in his officers would be the first step in losing control of his ship. And all this would happen during one of the greatest, most complex naval operations of all time.

Chapter 8
Mulberries & Whales

On the pebbly beaches of Northern France, a German Army photographer snapped pictures of an Allied failure. Trucks, tanks, small armored vehicles, and the bodies of English, Canadian, and American soldiers lie strewn across the wide crescent overlooked by steep chalky cliffs. The Allies began their attack with combined air, naval, and amphibious forces beginning at 5 AM. By 9 AM it was all over. Almost 60 percent of those who made it ashore were killed, wounded, or captured. The rest retreated back to England. It was an unmitigated disaster that spawned thousands of theories as to why it had failed. This was an alternative history to Normandy, two years before the famous Allied invasion: The Dieppe Raid of August 1942.

In so many ways, the raid's objectives were different from those of Normandy. First, it was not meant to push forward into Europe; only to hold a port city, collect intelligence, destroy key German emplacements, and get out. The invasion of Normandy was intended to retake Western Europe from Nazi control.

But there were valuable lessons from the operation. First, securing a port city would be almost impossible. Even with meager defenses at Dieppe (many German troops had been moved to the Eastern front where the Russians were advancing) the Allied landing suffered horrific losses. As few as 50 German soldiers defended some of the beaches around Dieppe.

Lessons from Dieppe were clear. To be successful in a full invasion, the Allies would have to accomplish several key elements. First, they would have to achieve a total surprise, not just in the time of the invasion but in its location. Secondly, the Allies would have to feed that invading army with men, supplies, and weapons to fight back against an almost certain counterattack.

Basically, the Allies needed what did not exist: a port that they could obtain with total surprise and minimal casualties, and could hold long enough to supply their armies. And, they would have to somehow prevent the Germans from destroying or disabling it in retreat.

The site for the landings was chosen not for its easy access to deep water harbors nor was it chosen because it was lightly defended. In fact, leading up to the attack, Rommel placed a perimeter of concrete bunkers and staked mines along beaches.

Normandy was considered a highly unlikely site for the invasion for a single reason: it could not easily and dependably be resupplied.

After an amphibious landing there, the highs and lows of the tides at Normandy would mean that a steady stream of heavy equipment would be impossible to maintain. Infantry that made it inland would be confronted by waves of tanks; even if the Allies managed to land, their tanks, fuel, and ammunition would soon run out. Holding onto anything more than a sliver of beach would be difficult. Pushing inland toward Paris and, eventually, Berlin would be impossible.

In May of 1944, British Intelligence personnel noticed something disturbing in the clues from crossword puzzles in the *Daily Telegraph*. Codes for the Normandy invasion were scattered through the puzzle. Words like Utah and Omaha and Mulberry weren't just amusing, quirky clues; they were codenames for key components to the upcoming invasion. One of the greatest military secrets of its time was essentially being broadcast to the public and the enemy. The *Telegraph* puzzle revealed more about the immensity of the project and how the Allies approached intelligence. D-Day was such a logistically enormous undertaking that keeping it a secret was almost impossible. Layers upon layers of misdirection were necessary to keep the truth hidden.

From false radio broadcasts to an entire false army complete with inflatable trucks, tanks, and airplanes presided over by a very real General Patton, one of the Allies biggest weapons in the war was deception. Sounds of tanks and trucks were broadcast into small British towns and false rumors spread by word of mouth. Generally, any tactic that could drown out the truth was used.

It is almost certain that somewhere in the transmissions, German spies picked up that the landing could be at the beaches of Normandy. However, Germany could not spread its already thin resources to cover all likely landing sites.

The puzzle leak wasn't a failure in intelligence. It actually proved that the layers of deception were working. It turned out that military personnel were using the code words loosely in conversation and were overheard by curious schoolboys who supplied the clues to the *Telegraph.* Against the chatter of background deception, it didn't matter that anyone knew the words Mulberry, Utah, or Omaha. Those words could be applied to the thousands of false truths being circulated.

The key to invading France was staring the Germans in the face in newsprint and on the beaches in Normandy. If the Allies couldn't seize a port, they would build one. And they would do it through Operation Mulberry: one of the largest operations from WWII and one of the least known.

It was not always a popular plan. Eisenhower himself described it as "a project so unique as to be classified by many scoffers as completely fantastic."

Winston Churchill had championed a similar idea during World War I in a plan that called for blocking the port of Zeebrugge by sinking ships across its channel. This plan was designed to outflank the German front as well as prevent a submarine base from being established there. It was actually one of many naval and amphibious plans designed to break out of the trench warfare that frustrated both sides during the war. Churchill had been part of a planned invasion of Denmark coordinated with Russian troops to seize the coasts, hem in the German navy, and bring the war close to Berlin.

For many in the military of 1914, the proposal may as well have been to invade the moon.

"It is quite mad...I have never read such an idiotic, amateur piece of work as this outline in my life..." was a typical response from Captain Herbert Richmond, the assistant director of operations on the Admiralty's Naval Staff during WWI.

In 1914, the British had the luxury of choosing not to attempt a complicated and risky amphibious assault. In 1944 the Allies had little choice. Delaying an attack further ran the risk of the Soviets negotiating a separate peace with Germany, ending the war in the East, and entrenching German control over mainland Europe. Even in Italy, where the Allies had landed in autumn of 1943, the fighting continued fiercely by the Germans. In fact, resistance there continued after the fall of Berlin. If the Western Allies were to see a true victory, they would have to breach Fortress Europe. It was first a question of where.

The selection of such an unlikely landing place as the Normandy coast made it perfect. Strong currents swept past the shoreline. The beaches sloped gradually out to sea, preventing ships with a large draft from accessing the shoreline. High and low tide varied greatly. In order for the Allies to land at Normandy and hold the beach, they would have to address these issues: build an artificial harbor to block the currents and create long jetties that would rise and fall with the tide so that large ships could quickly unload heavy trucks and tanks.

The entire port would have to be built practically overnight and under enemy attack from the shore, air, and sea. Even if the German spies had seen the crossword puzzle in the *Telegraph*, it's unlikely that they would have associated those code names with the operation or even guessed that Normandy was the target. The plan was simply too far-fetched to believe.

Building an artificial harbor here would have been difficult in the best of times with ideal weather conditions, months of planning, and a safe harbor to base construction operations.

But the reality was far more bleak. The Allies would have to build a harbor in Britain, tow it to a hostile shore only hours after initial beach landings, and construct a harbor while being shelled and attacked from the air.

It almost would take collective insanity to embark on such an unwieldy endeavor. Combat was one thing—men threw themselves into battle, jumped from airplanes, encased themselves in massive machines, and dug into trenches—but actually planning, engineering, and constructing a project in which so many things could go wrong was inviting failure. And yet this was precisely the plan the Allies pursued.

Churchill pushed through the plan against those dragging their feet: "Don't argue the matter. The difficulties will argue for themselves."

The British began planning for Mulberry in 1942, starting humbly by floating children's bath toys in a tub to illustrate how piers could rise and fall with the tides.

The harbor would consist of five elements. Whale units were causeways that floated on pontoons—essentially floating bridges that could carry trucks and tanks inland offloaded from large ships. Whale units were attached to Loebnitz piers, which were manually raised and lowered according to the tides. These piers would be where ships would offload equipment. Rather than floating freely on the water, these units could be adjusted according to the tide with a series of pulleys and winches. This ensured a relatively stable offloading point and somewhat stabilized the causeway floating on pontoons.

In order to create a break wall, the Allies employed several layers of protection. One was codenamed Gooseberries. These were old freighters and outdated warships sunk into the waters surrounding the beaches of Normandy. The Gooseberries provided some breakwater protection but a more solid structure was needed to create a sheltered harbor. This is where Phoenix units filled in.

Floating bridges and sunken ships were tough challenges, but the Phoenix units represented an entirely new level of engineering difficulty. These concrete units were caissons, a proven technology used in bridge building where a stone or concrete structure is sunken into the bed of a river, lake, or ocean. The rate of descent is controlled by flooding a compartment of air beneath the object until it submerges. The technology was used to build the Brooklyn Bridge where caissons were sunk into the bed of the East River and dug in deeper into the riverbed by men inside.

Normandy's caissons presented the additional difficulty of transportation. The objects needed to be towed across the English Channel, a challenge given their unwieldy size and construction. First of all, they were massive. Each was the height of a five-story building, several blocks long, and built in a similar rectangular shape. Phoenix units didn't cut through the water; they plowed through it, almost pulling against the efforts of the tugs tasked with getting them to France. Armed with AA guns and a crew, the Phoenix units were almost like a ship—a large, difficult-to-maneuver ship.

Edward Ellsberg, in his account of Operation Mulberry, *The Far Shore,* recounted the first time he saw the Phoenix units assembled off Selsey-Bill, a headland jutting into the English Channel near the Isle of Wight:

> *"What was this fantasy, sprawled over five square miles at least of what should be the rippling open sea? That conglomeration of tall black towers reaching skyward from beneath the Channel waters? That massive jumble of half sub-merged*

block-long windowless concrete warehouses—a hundred of them, perhaps even more—far and near protruding in no recognizable pattern, helter-skelter, from the waves?"

Ellsberg was no less awed by the site of the Whale units—the floating roadways that were to be used to unload tanks and trucks onto the beaches:

"Those ponderous steel arches, evidently disjointed sections of highway bridges, beginning nowhere, ending nowhere, mysterious swimming on the surface of the sea, somehow afloat in spite of gravity, interspersed crazily amongst the even crazier disarray of those semi-submerged concrete buildings? A city, perhaps insanely shuffled about and then sunk by some overwhelming catastrophe?"

"There it rested like a titanic unsolved jigsaw puzzle, scrambled beyond any recognition of its true design. Half-engulfed in the channel waters, it lay in a multitude of pieces, the instrument unenvisioned by the enemy (so we hoped), which was to sustain an invasion which the enemy High Command knew could not possibly be successfully sustained. Provided only, that as planned, we got it from Selsey Bill to the far Shore close on the heels of the first wave of our invaders."

Towing the large concrete Phoenix units was slow work as illustrated by Ellsburg when he crossed aboard one during the invasion:

"I crossed the Channel for the invasion of Normandy aboard a 6000-ton block of concrete at the end of a long towline, moving at all of three knots astern a laboring tug. The crossing took over thirty hours—no very swift passage. We—that is, the squadron of some ten similar chunks of concrete—had the protection of no convoy of our own, we were much too slow for any convoy to stay with us. But by keeping in the mainstream of invasion traffic bound for France, we had the benefit of the occasional presence in our vicinity of destroyers passing us accompanying faster groups, mainly troop carriers."

"Still, especially during the night passage, there was always the chance an E-boat might phase itself into the traffic lane, astern of one group of destroyers, ahead of the next, and take a shot at that Phoenix—it could hardly miss. We on a Phoenix had no more chance of taking evasive action to dodge a torpedo coming our way than had the Houses of Parliament in ducking a bomb. One Phoenix had already been so sunk the night before by an E-boat...."

"The net effect of all this on the thirty men, half Seabees and half soldiers, forming the crew of my Phoenix, was first to see our AA guns constantly manned for action. And secondly I noted that every man aboard, including myself, elected to sleep in the open on the topside, picking out the soft side of a hard plank on the wooden platform serving as a deck there, as far above the water as he could get,

and incidentally, with his Mae West cuddled closely alongside him."

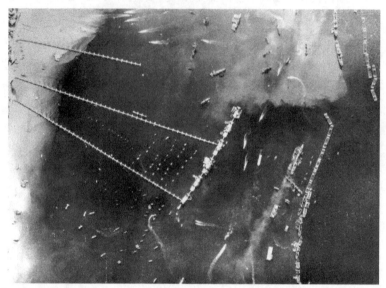

Aerial view of the Mulberry installation during the Normandy invasion

But despite its inherent complexities, Operation Mulberry's greater challenge was its bureaucratic management. The operation was becoming a debacle even before the invasion began. Construction of just about every element of the harbors was behind schedule, and there was constant bickering between Army and Navy command, as well as between British and American branches. To make matters worse, there was a constant shortage of men both to operate the various components of the harbor and to defend them against air attack. There was also a lack of tugs to move the components into place—in fact, the *Partridge* was one of only two ocean-going tugs capable of moving larger elements of Mulberry present in the region during early 1944.

At the same time that the *Partridge* arrived in Britain to report for duty with Mulberry, the entire operation came under a new command: Captain Dayton Clark. The appointment came after considerable haggling and bickering between British and American branches of the military, demonstrating the need for the kind of man they selected. Clark was a tough, administrative U.S. Naval officer with extensive experience working with the British fleet in combat operations in the Mediterranean. As the command of Mulberry (also known as CTF 128), Clark had authority over both the British and American military, often commanding officers that outranked him.

Clark was a hard-driving mid-level officer who would let nothing stop him from reaching his goal. By all accounts, the captain was single-minded in his goal: getting components to Normandy and assembling the harbor. Being well-liked was not in the job description, and Clark seemed completely and utterly unconcerned about achieving that goal.

But his gruff nature and laser-like focus had a purpose. Alfred Stanford, in his history *Force Mulberry,* describes how Clark's personality cut through politics and polite conversation making him *"an Ahab-like figure, feared, hated, resented and unpopular in both USN and RN circles, but respected by his staff of determined and isolated men."*

Operation Mulberry was one of the most administratively complicated tasks of the war. Clark reported to a myriad of superior officers, both Americans and British, all with their own opinions and priorities about resources and strategy. The result was that Clark was often left without equipment, men, and other resources to get the job done.

Clark didn't let incompetence get in his way either up the chain of command or down it. But his essential role in the invasion insulated him from normal military hierarchy. There are accounts of superior officers deferring their court marshals on him, knowing that they would only disrupt the operation.

He was clearly a man who was tough but he was also just the sort of man who didn't shy away from a harsh representation of his personality. In writing the book *Force Mulberry*, Stanford—who had served under Clark as a deputy commander—consulted heavily with Clark. Still, the book depicts Clark as a harsh taskmaster berating subordinates, driving men to exhaustion, and losing his temper at the slightest misstep of both those under his command and in the ranks above him. Clark insisted that those passages remain intact.

Clark's sunken eyes, haggard expression, and perpetual lack of sleep became emblematic of Force Mulberry under his command. The entire endeavor had millions of ways to fail and it was Clark's dogged determination that none of those ways would come to pass. His command represented everything challenging about naval command in an intensely concentrated form. Time was tight, the project was complex, and the stakes couldn't be higher. Clark was a man who seemed born for this moment. The coordination of one of the largest and most daring military operations of all time needed someone with dogged determination and a gruff, no-nonsense command style that won him admiration because everyone who worked under him knew that he had one goal in mind: victory at Normandy.

Clark's challenge was not just the planning for the invasion fleet but the construction and implementation of the harbor. This would give the ships ultimately serving under this command structure an extreme amount of independence. Superiors were less likely to be concerned about the conditions aboard a ship so long as it was operating in the theater. Clark may have been tough, but he was no micromanager. The more independent, the better.

Towing a massive object required that it be controlled both in the open water and in port. There was also the problem of constructing and running a harbor in a war zone.

Dayton Clark recognized these challenges and tapped into the civilian sector for help. He appointed Edward J. Moran as an admiral and gave him the duty of overseeing the tugs. Moran was the president of the Moran Towing Company in New York. The company was a fixture to any New Yorker who peered across the busy harbor at the tiny tugs darting in and out of cargo ships and cruise liners with large, white "M"s painted on their stacks. In fact, the Moran tugs can still be seen in New York and Boston today.

Moran was put in charge of all towing operations, American and British, that had anything to do with the installation of the harbors. The Allies had already completed a monumental task in constructing the harbor components that needed to be transported to France. Moran arrived to advise in the final stages of towing these elements across open water and potentially through rough seas. He was a man born into the life of harbor tugs. His family had started the company in the 1800s. He grew up working on tugboats, literally learning the ropes from his uncles and also learning the logistical coordination that it took to smoothly run a business amid the chaos of New York harbor.

The U.S. Navy needed Moran, and Clark had requested him several times. But the delay in appointing him to take charge of tugs for the operation points to the Navy's bias in using its own expertise.

In the end, even the Navy brass knew that, while its carrier task force was finding historic victory in the Pacific, it was a small fleet of tugs that would win the war at sea against Germany. Building the harbor on the far shore of Europe was the only way to infiltrate fortress Europe. And they would need Moran to coordinate the efforts as well as tugboat sailors like Joe Cooney to execute the plan.

Mulberry was mired in politics both between and within the two navies and armies that depended on its success. These politics were exasperated by ignorance: no one in any military had experience with a precision towing operation on this scale. Moran changed all that. Not only did he have the know-how, he had authority born of experience that was difficult to argue with. Both the British and Americans put a high degree of confidence in Moran and in the crews he supervised.

Operation Mulberry was unlike anything that had ever been attempted in the U.S. Navy. To military men accustomed to convoys, battle tactics, and even submarine warfare, Operation Mulberry resembled a large public works project more than it did a naval operation.

And, like many public works projects, it was competing for attention from politicians who controlled the purse strings. Moran was so desperate to acquire 200 tugs in late 1943 that he sent Deputy Commander of Force Mulberry, Cmdr. A. B. Stanford (who later wrote *Force Mulberry*) to Washington with a signed request from General Eisenhower himself. His task was to "steal, cadge, or persuade people to let go of tugs."

In the end, however, only 132 tugs were available for service on the eve of D-Day, of which 108 would be available for towing Phoenixes, Bombardons, and Whale Units. Stanford chalked out a grid on the headquarters in Portsmouth and used children's building blocks to represent tugs, moving them as the actual tugs crossed the channel. He wrote later in a memoir: "Each hour I would move the bricks and snap a picture. In the end, by simple counting, I could tell the number of tugs in the Channel at any hour of any day."

The world of Moran was the world in which Boatswain Joe Cooney had lived and thrived. Rough men operating in all weather doing the unglamorous work of wrangling, pushing, and pulling some of the largest manmade objects ever created: These were the men shipping thousands of pounds of freight in and out of harbors up and down the East Coast. While passenger liners, warships, and freighters cut smoothly through the water and ships maintained a spit and polish image on their decks, it was the tugs that faced the grimy hard work of getting them safely into and out of the harbor.

But despite its appearance as a construction project, Operation Mulberry was very much operating in a combat zone. The dangers in the waters around Britain were real even before the invasion began. In April, a training exercise, Operation Tiger, was attacked by nine German E-boats. E-boats were actually the designation by the Allies, short for Enemy Boats. The Germans called them Schnellboot or Fast Boats. It was a simple but apt name. The craft could top off at 48 knots or 55 mph. They were specifically designed to travel through the notoriously rough seas of the English Channel and Baltic Sea. Armed with torpedoes, the ships could strike quickly and avoid a counter attack. During WWII they sank 101 merchant ships, 12 destroyers, 11 minesweepers, eight landing ships, six tugs, a torpedo boat, a minelayer, one submarine, and various small merchant craft. They also damaged two cruisers, five destroyers, three landing ships, a repair ship, a naval tug, and numerous merchant vessels.

During Operation Tiger eight landing ships were attacked by these small, deadly craft. The fast boats managed to hit two of the troop ships with torpedoes near Plymouth and Dartmouth. They then strafed the decks of the burning ships and fired on survivors jumping into the sea. A total of 749 soldiers and sailors were killed in the attack.

And if the crews on ships like the *Partridge* didn't know the danger they were in, German propaganda reminded them. Broadcasts by the English-speaking (and accented) "Lord Haw-Haw" had a significant impact on the morale of the soldiers and sailors working on Mulberry. While troops on both sides of the war in Europe seemed soothed by the German love song 'Lili Marlene', Allies were unsettled by the details that the enemy seemed to know about the operation. Ellsberg conveys the uneasy feeling at the end of the day working on a "secret" operation under the nose of the enemy.

> *"After 'Lili Marlene' as usual had put all her listeners into a trance, came Lord Haw-Haw, to jolt at least all those involved in Operation Mulberry rudely back to reality with his personal greeting:"*

> *"'To those United States Navy Seabees and soldiers on the concrete caissons off Selsey Bill.'"*

"We know exactly what you intend to do with those concrete units. You think you are going to sink them on our coasts in the assault. Well, we are going to help you boys. We'll save you the trouble. When you come to get underway, we're going to sink them for you."

If the Germans could make a disaster out of a simple rehearsal for the invasion, what would they do to the real thing when they seemed to know the details of the top-secret operation?

As part of Operation Mulberry, the *Partridge* sailed into a perfect storm combining the deteriorating conditions aboard, lack of higher authority and oversight, and an extremely challenging mission.

In the winter of 1944, Joe Cooney was sailing in familiar waters. Not only was he helping the *Partridge* acclimate to close harbor and towing work as part of Operation Mulberry, but he was back in Britain. It was a country he had not seen since the Great War. Time had inevitably changed the place, but so had war. Throughout the country, buildings lay in ruin from the German bombing campaign, and the besieged country was not expending precious resources rebuilding yet. In a letter home to Florie, Cooney related seeing Britain again after serving time there during WWI:

Saturday, February 5, 1944

Dear Florie,

Just a few lines to let you know I'm still alive and well. Hope all the family are in good health and getting along alright....I'm kept pretty busy now more so than ever before, I have the whole ship to take care of again and it sure keeps me hopping. You know by now where I am. Same place as before. My old stomping ground but it isn't the same, they sure raised hell here and are still at it. I visited some of the places I used to go to when I was a kid and they were all wiped out...

At this point in the war, Britain was a place of in betweens. Not home, but not totally foreign. A country at war but not quite the front line.

With a mix of cultures, a war-torn infrastructure, pub brawls, and encounters with the opposite sex, life on shore reflected both the excitement and dangers of a wartime country recounted in books and films from and about the era. There was also life on the water. The crew of the *Partridge* wasn't simply waiting for the invasion to happen or even preparing for it; she was constantly busy with duties moving through the maze of watercraft surrounding the British coastline.

The waterways in and around Britain were swollen with everything the Allies would need to go to war. The massive armada that would spearhead the coming invasion joined troop and cargo transportation from the U.S. plus the heavy ship traffic needed to move goods around the island itself. Major ports in the United States may have seen large numbers of ships leaving their harbors. But in 1944, on the eve of D-Day, British waterways would have bordered on chaotic.

The *Partridge* found itself cruising as part of convoys towing in and out of unfamiliar ports like Portsmith, Tilbury, and Sesley-Bill. The crew, accustomed to working on salvage operations, suddenly found a tighter schedule in waters that required far more attention. Pilots from the British Navy would guide the ship out to sea and back in again—requiring more protocol, paperwork, and an overall level of bureaucracy that hadn't been part of daily life in the Caribbean.

Joe Cooney would have been most familiar with the kind of close harbor work that the *Partridge* now participated in. But even for Joe, the Mulberry operation was daunting.

The *Partridge* was involved in towing the components of Mulberry from construction ports to staging areas. This served the practical purpose of putting the pieces in place for the invasion as well as training the crew in towing the caissons across the Channel after the initial D-Day invasion.

This type of command structure should have been ideal for the *Partridge,* given her operating history in the Caribbean. But the ship sailing into Britain that winter was far different from the one that had served in the warm blue water dotted with islands.

In fact, things had gone from bad to worse aboard the *Partridge* before any operations began for Mulberry. Shortly after arriving in Britain, Caldin's chilly relationship with his officers had frozen solid. The officers thought it was strange that Caldin refused to dine with them when he first took command, but now he barely spoke to them and they did their best to avoid contact with him. Orders were often written and handed to officers or left for them to be found. And the content of the orders was often stranger than their format. Many of the officers began to take issue with Caldin's capricious orders that often ran in the face of efficiently running the ship. A disheveled sailor performing an essential task would often be berated by Caldin as the officer in charge would either helplessly stand by and watch or step in and defend the sailor and then suffer the consequences.

Caldin created a chalkboard with two columns placing officers "in hoc" and "out of hoc," presumably to note which officers were supporting his command and which were not. One officer apparently "out of hoc" often in the early days was Lt. Thomas Buffum, a Brown University graduate and Quaker from Rhode Island. Buffum was tall, good looking, had a beautiful singing voice, and gained an instant rapport with both officers and enlisted men. He represented everything that had eluded Caldin, and he became an early target for the captain's ridicule. Buffum was "confined to ship for five days for disobedience of a lawful order of the Commanding Officer." Just three days later, the same punishment was handed to Buffum. Then on the January 19, only six days later, Buffum was suspended from duty for "disrespectful deportment to his superior officer while in the execution of his office."

During this same period of time, Caldin held no fewer than four deck courts to punish sailors for arriving late over leave and drunk and disorderly conduct. Each infraction received Caldin's preferred punishment: reduction in rank and pay.

In a different theater of war or a different duty, the *Partridge* may have been more closely observed. Even a stressful combat situation would have more command structure than Operation Mulberry.

But the ship was sailing into uncharted territory by participating in the early days of Mulberry. The unwieldy Mulberry operation needed a ship with extensive towing experience, but the ship also needed a commander who would follow the advice and counsel of his officers. Furthermore, unlike many other naval operations, the *Partridge* would be working in an extremely independent fashion. A direct chain of command existed but its members were often occupied with ensuring that Mulberry would receive enough support and less apt to look at the performance and condition of one ship that it already counted as its own. In other words, the command structure didn't break down during this operation, but it operated differently than it normally would have. And for Adnah Caldin, this may have been the difference between his success and failure as a captain.

Chapter 9
The Navy Man and Tug Boat Captain

On March 11, 1919, the USS *Auk* limped into Boston Harbor. On her way to clear the minefield known as the Great Barrage in the North Sea, the newly commissioned *Auk* began taking on water during a severe storm. Between New York and Boston, the water inside the hull reached a critical point and the captain ordered her to pull into Boston as a safe harbor.

A young sailor, barely 17 years old, stepped off the *Auk* and ended his career in the Navy. He had sailed to France aboard the USS *Christabel* while the First World War still was blazing in Europe, seen action with German U-boats, and had witnessed an officer heroically disable a jammed depth charge, actions that would earn him the Medal of Honor. The young sailor was Adnah Caldin, a thin, bespectacled boy with hair parted down the center. He looked like he would be more at home as an office clerk or on a college campus than aboard a naval vessel.

And that was the idea. For the time being, he was done with war and the United States Navy. Staring at a poster for the Mount Hermon School, Caldin dreamed of a better life. A return to his hometown of Tidioute, and the rowdy life in the hotel and saloon his father owned, wasn't an option.

But joining the Navy and heading to war didn't turn out to be the escape hatch Caldin was searching for. Most of the officers came from privileged backgrounds with college degrees at a time when the majority of Americans did not have a high school diploma.

Mount Hermon was a leg up into a better life. After graduation, there would be college. Maybe Harvard or Yale. Then, a life in New York or Washington, D.C. and perhaps a career as a journalist. These were the dreams that Adnah Caldin set off to pursue that day. And he would be helped by powerful and wealthy family friends.

A parallel journey also began in the WWI Navy with another young sailor destined to cross paths with Caldin: Joe Cooney. Cooney and Caldin were close in age and in their early experience in WWI (Cooney had also served in the Navy toward the end of the war.) But Joe Cooney's life took a different turn. He had no powerful wealthy friends, and private schools and universities never even occurred to him. He loved the water and returned to it in civilian life in the harbors of New York City, plunging himself into the gritty dock life that was a steady paycheck: a life set against a spider web of tugs and ferries crisscrossing the busiest harbor in the world.

Cooney and Caldin are a snapshot of American lives between the wars. The story of the USS *Partridge* would be tidier if one man came from a privileged background and the other working class. It would be a simpler tale if one man had extensive experience at sea and the other had none.

But Adnah Caldin and Joe Cooney both came from modest means, and both worked hard to make a better life for themselves and their families. Both were veterans of The Great War and both had extensive experience aboard ships. Their stories are a complex mixture of ambition, the dynamics of leadership, and ultimately, performance under pressure. And both of their lives would eventually intertwine aboard the *Partridge.*

Joe Cooney's rank during WWII was Chief Boatswain. A ship's Boatswain (pronounced Bo 'sun) is one of the oldest named ranks in the military. The derivation of the name belies its importance aboard a ship. The word comes from a combination of Old English and Old Norse. "Batt" meaning boat and Sveinn meaning young man. The term basically meant a servant or follower. In the modern U.S. Navy, however, the term meant anything but a boy or servant.

A boatswain's duties reflect its ancient heritage; in the past the role focused on handling the ship's lines so crucial to controlling sails. Boatswains also traditionally organized and executed an abandon ship order.

A ship's boatswain in a WWII-era ship was in charge of the rigging, the care and maintenance of her lifeboats, anchoring, mooring, and towing. The rank oversaw basically the operations at sea-requiring a knowledge not just of how a ship moves through the water but how it interacts with other objects. A boatswain would know the intricate play between objects at sea that don't always move in relationship with each other in an intuitive manner. The laws of action and reaction are more pronounced in the water and the tug and pull of objects often results in an unexpectedly complex, slow-motion ballet. This dance most often takes place in the harbor, where usually a ship's boatswain's duties are focused—docking, anchoring, running lines to tugs—all the actions that allow a ship to push and pull or be pushed and pulled with grace.

In this way, the boatswain handled the realities of a ship's life. A captain could engage an enemy, an executive officer could order a course, but a boatswain had to negotiate the realities of physics—lines that stretched and contracted and water that rose and fell. And ships that no longer held their crew.

For the most part, World War II's great battles were fought and won by the actions of captains—decisive men who put their ships, their men, and themselves in harm's way. Modern war at sea hurled massive shells miles across the ocean, sent swarms of airplanes against fleets of ships, and often saw great battleships serving as artillery platforms for land battles.

But these battles were only a small fraction of how a global navy operates and the vast infrastructure that supported these decisive battles was often manned by ship's boatswains, who took care of the towing, target practice, tethering, and anything else the Navy deemed "unusual" seamanship operations. With the exception of abandon ship procedures, unusual seamanship operations rarely took place in a line of battle. It isn't that the Navy didn't respect the role of boatswain, but it never gave the role a level of importance in a combat situation. That all changed with Operation Mulberry.

Mulberry required the Navy to view its primary function—battle at sea—as secondary to an engineering and towing operation. Massive numbers of tugs would move from England to France across some of the longer stretches of the channel and assemble a harbor. The rigging, line handling, and coordination of crews would place the role of ship's boatswain as a central figure in a major naval operation.

Cooney's work in the New York City harbor was ideal preparation for the *Partridge* during its ramp up to D-Day. In one of the most crowded harbors in the world, Cooney skippered tug boats and served as the wheelman working for railroad companies from the mid-twenties until he rejoined the Navy in 1943. But career cultivation was not part of Cooney's world. His life on the water was hard work, pure and simple. Romantic notions about adventures on the high seas or a nobel officer class didn't fit into life on the waters that Cooney sailed in.

Joe Cooney while serving in the Navy during WWI

Cooney gained his experience on the job at a slow and steady pace between the wars. He worked for the Pennsylvania Railroad Maritime Division from October 1928 to May 1938, starting as a deckhand working his way up as a master pilot on NY Harbor tugs. He worked for the Erie Railroad Co., Marine Division from May 1938 to August 1942 as a wheelman and pilot of the ferry *Meadville* running between lower Manhattan and Hoboken, NJ. The *Meadville* was known for her speed and maneuverability. A Uniflow engine allowed the ship to respond rapidly from full ahead to full astern, making it highly effective in the right hands, but tricky to many skippers.

Raymond Baxter described the *Meadville* in *Stories of a Deckhand* as a ship that was powerful but unpredictable:

> *"During her time on the Erie roster, the Meadville did a lot of damage. They say she was a good boat for speed, one of the fastest on the river. She could also make a fool out of unsuspecting captains. She was a boat that you had to master and keep a wary eye on."*

Baxter recounted the schooling he received in steering a ferryboat from Tommy Hogan, a skipper of the *Meadville* in the late 1940s and early 1950s. His passages on working the river reveal a world of tough, rugged men who took seriously their role in imparting knowledge upon younger men. An apprentice-like system existed that Joe Cooney would have been exposed to working his way up from a deckhand. Baxter recounts the first time he piloted the *Meadville* across the Hudson River:

> *"Tom stood directly behind the steering wheel, watching the sheer pole. Tom would say, 'Ease her up, don't let her come around too fast,' or 'Use less wheel,' or other quiet little orders. About halfway*

across the river, Tom would say, 'Okay, Son, I'll take her from here.' Believe me, was I disappointed! Each night, that 'Okay, Son, I'll take her' came later and later. Till about the fifth night, it happened: I left Chambers Street and Tom was giving me little pointers and we got closer and closer and still closer, but no 'Okay, Son, I'll take her.' All he kept doing was telling me just what to do, I started to get a little scared as I thought to myself, 'When is he going to take this boat?...Boy, we're getting awful close to the dock and boy, it sure looks big...I hope he knows what he's doing, because I don't.' But Tom just kept saying, 'Bring her around a little more, that's good, not too much wheel, Okay, slow your boat down, bring her around now keep her between the clumps, okay, stop your boat.' Then just as the bow of the Tuxedo came abreast of the clumps at the end of the rack, Tom said 'Go Back [full stern]...Give her the next back just about halfway in the slip to kill some more of the way.' When we were just about up to the bridge, Tom said, 'Give her a quick back...Slow ahead...Half ahead...Okay, when she's all tied up, stop your boat and ring the cowbell.' After I did that, Tom said, 'Well, that's it. You just took your first ferryboat across the river.'"

It was aboard ships like the *Meadville* that Cooney learned his craft. In Baxter's recollection from the 1940s *Meadville,* you can hear echoes of "Sail Easy" Kenney and Lt. Snipes. Cooney played the same role on the *Partridge* with the younger sailors and even the officers who stood above him in rank but didn't question his experience.

Cooney's life at sea was a day job. No long excursions kept him away for weeks or even months at a time. He had a wife and together they raised a family of four in some of the tougher neighborhoods of Queens. But Cooney was the epitome of the tough Irishman who loved a good fight as much as he loved a good laugh.

His son, Patrick Cooney, was 12 years old when his father went off to war a second time. His memories paint a picture of a man who cared deeply for his family, but was quick to instill self-sufficiency in his children.

"When I was about 6, I was returning home from the grocery store with a loaf of bread I was sent to get, this was in the Borough of Queens, Long Island. I was jumped by 5 neighbor boys who ripped the bread out of my hands and started to beat on me. I took off running and crying when my dad, who observed the incident from the third-floor window, yelled at me to go back and kick their asses or he would kick mine! Still crying and fearful, I went back to what I feared least and flailed my fists at the gang until they ran away. My dad didn't praise my efforts; I recalled he said, 'Don't let me catch you running away from a fight again.'"

"Sometime later, in the same rough neighborhood, I was carrying a 10 cent pail of beer, which is how beer was carried out of bars, to my dad who was sitting on the front steps of our tenement, when a 19 yr. old bike rider purposely ran the bike into my back, literally knocking me head over heels. Of course, the beer pail went flying too and spilled its contents all over. Looking up from the ground I saw

the biker peddling away as fast as he could with my dad in hot pursuit; the biker wasn't fast enough and I saw my dad grab his collar and jerked him off the bike and proceed to punch the hell out of him, knocking him unconscious. I never was sure what angered my dad the most, my hurt or the loss of beer."

The lessons were clear—life was cruel, unfair, and someone was out to take advantage of you around every corner. You had to stand up for yourself. It was a lesson that Cooney had learned time and again in the streets of New York as well as within the rough and tumble world of its docks and harbors. It was a world that respected muscle and good humor more than brains or rank. And Joe Cooney could provide both.

In 1940, Cooney moved his family to a modestly middle-class neighborhood on Staten Island. The tree-lined streets were perfect on warm nights to sit outside with his family telling stories of his exploits during the war and characters he met on the docks and harbors of New York. But the family man still had the devilish Irish humor. Once, as a prank, he taught all of his kids curse words in reverse, delighting in their cries of "You Bon-of-a-Stitch!" and "You Bousy-Lastard!" One day his six-year-old daughter, who had a habit of reversing words, greeted him coming home with "You Son-of-a-Bitch!" and "You Lousy Bastard." Joe had to run down the block, scoop her up in his arms, and whisk her inside. Joe also had to visit every neighbor on the block and apologize for his backfired joke.

If Joe was perfectly suited for the job of a ship's boatswain, he was equally well suited for his role in civilian life. He was tough and no-nonsense, but he was also easy going. He loved his kids. He loved his wife. He was a good guy to know on the block. Someone to look after you. In other words, Joe Cooney was exactly the figure that young men shipping off to war need.

When the war broke out, Cooney didn't hesitate to sign up. But the Navy was choosing carefully then. Cooney was turned down several times. Too old. Too many dependents. But he had experience. He had a master license to captain any vessel under 2,500 tons and to pilot any vessel at any tonnage in the bays and sounds and rivers in and around New York. He knew how to move big things in congested waters. Waters beginning to form in the minds of D-Day planners.

And maybe it was one of these planning committees that sent out the word for men who knew a thing or two not about traditional naval combat, but about towing and tugging. As the details began to pile up, it became clear that the Navy had scant few men who had the experience to deal with the slow-motion ballet of constructing a harbor off the beaches of Normandy. And even fewer who would do it in a combat situation.

He was finally accepted as Warrant Boatswain in the USNR on January 9, 1943.

In finding Cooney, the Navy brass was solving one detail in an incredibly complex operation, but the *Partridge* was gaining something much more essential.

For Joe Shannon, Cooney seemed to embody not just the image of a father, but of his actual father.

"The first time I came aboard the ship I see this guy and I'm thinking 'what's my father doing on the ship?' That was the first time I saw Joe Cooney. I joined the navy looking for my Dad and I found him!"

While Joe was happy to receive the rank of Boatswain, Adnah Caldin was trying desperately to be promoted from the rank.

Caldin's life had been a series of false starts beginning with his departure from his hometown of Tidioute. In a request to Mount Hermon to complete his high school education he wrote:

"Having observed the advancement of men mostly college students or graduates to petty and commissioned officers in preference to others, I realized the necessity of an education in the Navy as well as in civilian life..."

Caldin may have been seeking education outside the Navy, but he clearly hoped to gain access to the officer class within it. His experience aboard the *Christabel* provided at least one role model in Ensign Sullivan, but he was frustrated at the barriers that existed for a young man without a high school education. Caldin returned to Tidioute and applied for schools to get his diploma and begin life as a student.

Tidioute is a small town on the Western edge of the Allegheny Forest and the site of some of the first commercial oil drilling in the country. In fact, after oil was first struck in nearby Titusville on August 27, 1859, news spread to Tidioute when a Colonel Robinson stopped at a general store owned by Samuel Grandin. His son, 22-year-old John L. Grandin, overheard the news and set off to search for oil on his own. Grandin became the second person to strike oil in the area. That well eventually failed, but Grandin doggedly pursued ventures in oil, eventually finding wealth in the transportation of oil through pipelines. His partner in many of these ventures was a man named Adnah Neyhart.

Adnah Caldin's father, John, had attended school with the Grandin Brothers as well as with Adnah Neyhart (the namesake of his future son Adnah Neyhart Caldin). But the oil money flowed past him.

His friends were men of means. Wealthy from the Pennsylvania oil boom, the Grandins and Neyhart had reaped the rewards from their considerable risks. And yet, somehow their good fortune had not rubbed off on John Caldin.

John Caldin was the owner and operator of the Hotel Caldin, and seemed to be an influence that family and friends were eager to distance young Adnah from. Whether it was the alcoholic tendencies of the senior Caldin or the unsavory surrounding of the hotel (which seemed to double as a casino and brothel), many people conspired to get Adnah out of town. Even prior to WWI, there was a major effort on the part of his mother and family friends to move the boy east to a school. And young Adnah had some powerful allies to make that happen.

The Mount Hermon School was selected because of its mission for taking in those with limited access to education. In a letter to the Mount Hermon dated April 15, 1916, John R. Hague, secretary to John Grandin, spells out the relationship the Caldins had with the Grandin brothers and Adnah Neyhart:

> *"J. L. Grandin knows the boy and his father well, and would, I am sure, willingly endorse his application. The boy and his mother will be tremendously disappointed if you cannot take him. If you cannot take him as a boarder this fall, could*

he board outside till the opening of the winter term?
The boy is named after another cousin of J.L.G's,
Adnah Neyhart of Boston and Framingham. The
father, John Caldin, was a schoolmate here of both
J.L.G., A.N. and my brothers Will and Elliott, hence
their interest. It will be the making of him."

The correspondence with the Mount Hermon School also indicated that J.L. Grandin's interest in the young Adnah Caldin extended beyond namesakes:

"He is smart and well worth saving from the snares
of the village hotel which his father owns and runs.
Adnah wants to go very much, and is to meet me
here at the office this afternoon for a conference.
His mother came to my sister-in-law's home last
evening for a conference with us. She will
undertake the boy's support, as she is greatly
distressed re the father's attitude in the matter, as
well as the influences of the barroom loafers."

In another letter written a month later, Hague pleads with a Professor Cutler:

"If his papers are satisfactory can you not consider
him for the fall? I do hope so, for his father keeps a
bar and is cruel at times to Adnah."

"The boy has $400, which he has saved up, but he
had gotten in with the poolroom gangs here,
become discouraged and lost his ambition. A friend
and I have had several talks with him, and now he
has taken a good start in the right direction, had
forsaken the old crowd, is deeply interested in

Hermon, and has set his heart on going there this fall, if at all possible. He is a bright fellow, and will make a smart man if brought under the proper influences."

But despite these pleas, Caldin did not enter Mt Hermon that fall. Almost a year to the day that the last letter from John Hague was sent, the U.S. declared war on Germany and entered the war. Like many young men in previous wars, Caldin answered patriotic duty and sought a new life beyond Tidioute, as he later reflected in his application to Mount Hermon:

"I was born in Tidioute, PA, Oct 7, 1900, and have always lived here and attended school until December 21, 1917, when under a patriotic impulse, I ran away from home and school and enlisted in the U.S. Navy."

Perhaps that patriotic impulse left Caldin after the war ended or maybe he simply saw no further opportunity in the Navy, but he did return to school in the fall of 1919, attending Mount Hermon and, later, Philips Exeter. With bouts of travel interspersed, Caldin never earned a diploma from either school and reentered the Navy as a Seaman in 1924. He remained a sailor until 1933 when he "made rate" or, in other words, was promoted to Petty Officer 3rd class and given a job specialty. In Caldin's case, it was Boatswain. From 1933 to 1939, Caldin's career showed the ambitions of a young, hungry officer ready to ascend a career ladder in the Navy, education be damned. He was promoted to Boatswain's Mate 2nd Class, then to Boatswain's Mate 1st class, and then to Chief Petty Officer by 1939. Making

CPO in six years (1933-39) was exceptional—especially in the interwar Navy when promotion was very slow. At that time, CPO was the highest enlisted rank one could achieve.

A photo of Adnah Caldin taken while attending Philips Exeter, probably around 1919

Like many men during WWII, Caldin saw his opportunity for advancement increase significantly. In 1942, Caldin was given a temporary rank of lieutenant junior grade and then lieutenant senior grade. It was a rank in the Navy and in his life that, after so much struggle, he was determined to make permanent.

Cooney and Caldin's pathways to the *Partridge* could not have been more different: one was that of an ambitious career-minded Navy man and the other of an experienced hand and captain of ferries and tugs in a busy harbor. For one, the *Partridge* was a longed-for chance to serve his country one last time; for the other, it was a stepping stone to a higher rank and command of a larger ship.

But for all their differences, there were similarities. Both were veterans of WWI. They both clearly had a strong sense of duty to their country and many years of experience at sea. They also both had wives and children at home. Cooney had three young children and Caldin a six-year-old daughter. Unlike the mostly young kids serving as officers and sailors, Cooney and Caldin were middle-aged men sailing into combat with the most experience and, perhaps, the most to lose.

Chapter 10
Collision At Sea

"Sailor, tuck in that shirt! Failure to wear a regulation uniform! Failure to address a commanding officer in the proper manner!"

Caldin turned to Lt. Lefavor who stood by as he continued to dress down the young sailor who had been working on an engine repair.

"Mr. Lefavor, we will address this at a Captain's mast."

Lefavor exchanged looks with Buffum. It was just another typical day serving under Caldin.

No one was going to fault Caldin for running a tight ship, particularly in a time of war. These were days when harsh discipline matched harsh realities. Life-or-death actions depended on a coordinated, disciplined crew. In his mind, Caldin was like many commanders he served under. Hard-nosed, by-the-book, and uncompromising. In fact, with so many new recruits and officers with no previous military experience, a strong, experienced hand was necessary to slap a crew into shape to get the job done.

There was clearly no doubt in Caldin's mind that the *Partridge* had an inexperienced crew and a group of officers incapable of whipping them into shape. In his view, this collection of "90-day wonders" would learn from an experienced naval officer about the real way to run a ship.

Caldin's doubts about crew discipline were not unfounded. Most recruits had little or no experience at sea and the ship's time in the Caribbean, while an active combat tour, was not the massive and complex invasion armada that lay ahead. There may have been some truth that, for the most part, the officers and sailors aboard the *Partridge* were not fully prepared for the challenges that the operation off Normandy would throw at them.

But in the opinion of the officers and crew, it was Caldin who was unprepared. Caldin was unable to grasp the importance of fellow officers in supporting his command. A captain with little sea experience can depend on those under him for that knowledge. A captain uncomfortable relating to 'old salts' can rely on officers or senior crew members to bridge that divide. Even a captain with unreasonably high standards can rely on officers to improve crew behavior or skills to meet those demands and temper expectations.

Had Caldin merely tried his best to lead the ship on its mission and failed, the experienced crew and officers would have more than adequately covered the basics of maneuvering the ship and staying clear of danger. Men like Cooney certainly had the background for that. And men like Bill Ames knew the character of the crew and the capabilities of the ship.

This was not a case of poor leadership; it was a far more complex and dangerous evolution. It was a captain's alienation from the crew and officers in the midst of isolation and war.

Bizarre directives were issued almost daily from the captain, often in the form of a memo handed to an officer who would then have to enforce them. Struggling to justify the use of telescopes, drill daily "battle plans," and turn over the ship's galley for foodstuff inventories, the officers did their best but often ran afoul of Caldin for non-compliance with an order.

Even officers were not spared the scrutiny of Caldin on a daily basis.

Tom Buffum took to avoiding Caldin in the narrow passages of the small ship, ignoring orders that were impossible for the crew to achieve. The ship's log recorded the results:

10 January 1944:

Ensign T. B. BUFFUM, Jr., USNR, confined to ship for five days for disobedience of a lawful order of the Commanding Officer.

13 January 1944:

Ensign T. B. BUFFUM Jr., USNR, confined to ship for five days for disobedience of a lawful order of the Commanding Officer.

19 January 1944

Ensign T. B. BUFFUM, Jr. USNR suspended from duty for disrespectful deportment to his superior officer while in the execution of his office.

Then later that same day:

Ensign T. B. BUFFUM, Jr. USNR was restored to duty.

Tom Buffum and Frank Lefavor.

This pattern of discipline followed by reprieve was repeated often aboard the *Partridge* during this time. Lt. Ayers seemed to take over from Buffum for least favored officer:

On February 28, 1944

Lt. (jg) P. E. Ayers, USNR was confined to quarters for a period of five days for failure to carry out the directive contained in paragraph 4 of Commanding Officer's letter to Lt. (jg) P.E. Ayers, dated 18 January 1944.

The next day, Ayers received a reprieve:

March 1, 1944

Lt. (jr) P.E. Ayers, USNR, was released from confinement to quarters by commanding officer.

March 28, 1944

Ensign M. B. Rich, Jr., USNR, was confined to quarters for conduct unbecoming an officer, by the order of the Commanding Officer.

Many officers, like Mike Rich, came to the Navy directly from college, a major annoyance to Caldin who had earned his rank over a long period of time.

In this sense, Caldin's behavior seems to have a reason behind it. After all, a thin separation in rank did little to hide the years of experience in the Navy and at sea he had accumulated. In his own opinion, if there was anyone aboard who knew how to run a ship, it would have been Adnah Neyhart Caldin.

In addition to these disciplinary actions against officers, regular crew were also punished, usually having their rank reduced for minor infractions. Mike Rich recalled that friction with the Captain often came in defense of sailors unfairly maligned. The officers, many of whom were sailing on their first ship at sea, were beginning to openly question some of Caldin's more audacious orders: using outdated Naval customs, punishing sailors for minor uniform infractions, and questioning everything from towing procedures to how coffee should be made. Officers and senior crew members, while not disobeying Caldin outright, started to make their opinions known.

"If he was messing with a group of my guys, I let him know," recalled Mike Rich. "But, in the end, there wasn't much you could do. You'd all end up getting punished."

Caldin dealt with friction with the officers the same way he did with any problem: more discipline. It was at this point that Caldin began to keep his board with officer's names listing them as "In Hoc" and "Out of Hoc." They were called into long conferences sometimes lasting four or five hours, hashing and rehashing elements of the *Partridge* far from her immediate duties. Officers were increasingly alarmed at what they saw as a detriment to their real mission: serving as a work ship for the invasion of Europe.

Bill Ames, who was Master at Arms at the time, had the unpleasant duty of overseeing the unfair punishments of many of his crew mates. As one of the longest-serving men aboard the *Partridge*, Ames was horrified at the treatment the men were receiving. Reduction in rank meant a reduction in pay, which had a very real impact on the men. In addition, Ames could see a steady erosion of crew morale, a dangerous situation going into a war zone.

Meanwhile, Mike Rich was exhausted by countless meetings reviewing battle plans for the ship, all the time faced with the more immediate and challenging task of towing Mulberry and Whale units in the crowded waters around Britain.

What had started as a captain sterner than some others was becoming a dangerous combination of incompetence and absurdity. Don Wampler, who carried a wicked sense of humor throughout the war, wrote a poem about the crew's mounting anxiety about their commander:

YOU NAME IT – WE'RE AT A LOSS

Once there was a crazy guy-
Who thought that he was Captain Bligh?
He said, "We'll fight to our last cartridge"
He's known as the Feuher on the good ship
* "Partridge"*
He makes you work like a cornered rat,
And threatens to hit you with a baseball bat.
He thinks we're gladiators in a great arena,
If you think I'm foolin'—ask Messina!
The bridge is a hell-uv-a place to be
When the Captain goes on a spree.
He chases us off the bridge, so much
If you don't believe me—just ask Dutch!
When everyone is on the bridge
We like to watch the Captain fidge'
Then he throws you off in pairs
If you don't believe me—ask Mr. Ayers!
"Your Navigation is always wrong!"
He keeps on singing that same old song.
If it's not the quartermaster that he blames
It's someone else's—ask Mr. Ames!
Another thing that all of us hate
Is when he asks us "What's your rate?"
If this keeps up we'll all be looney,
If you think I'm lying—ask Mr. Cooney!
"Shoot 'em down, they don't belong up there!"
Then he starts to pull his hair
He thinks that there's no one braver,
Don't take my word—as Mr. Lefavor!
He'll bust you for the smallest thing,
We have to 'snap it" when he rings,
We all think that he's just a meany,

If you don't' believe me—just ask Feeny!
He'll always hum and tap a finger,
For a screwball he's a ringer.
The ship's morale is steadily flunkin'
If you think I'm kidding—just ask Duncan!
Hitler said "I Own the World and Space,"
But this guy's runn' him a Dammed Close Race!

The crew reacted to Caldin's treatment in sometimes immature, almost schoolboyish ways. One crewmember recalled being reprimanded for offering him weak coffee. He replenished the cup with an incredibly strong brew, which the Captain drank heartily declaring: "Now that's how you make a cup of coffee."

Bill Ames also recalled the engineering room conspiring with the bridge crew to substitute a reverse order with a full steam ahead, resulting in a dock collision in Britain.

More than anything, the officers and senior enlisted men were acutely aware that morale aboard the ship was slipping. At a low point, on March 29, James Ridpath attempted suicide by drinking phenol. He was sent to a hospital ashore and survived. His condition was more than likely irritated by the stress aboard his ship, but the suicide attempt became just one more story about life aboard the *Partridge* that sailors were telling with alarming frequency.

Shortly after this incident, another sailor was punished by being locked and chained below deck while the ship was under sail—a blatant violation of Navy regulations for safety reasons. Buffum, Rich, and Ames protested and were confined to quarters and stripped of their duties. More reductions in rank. More reductions in pay. A bigger rift between the captain of the *Partridge* and the crew.

The drama unfolding aboard the *Partridge* would have, more than likely, gone unnoticed if it didn't coincide with the faltering performance of the ship during a crucial stage of the war.

In early 1944, a series of collisions and towing mishaps began to highlight that something was terribly wrong aboard the ship.

In a memo to the Commander of the Twelfth fleet and the Bureau of Ships, Caldin casually refers to damage from the towing the ship had been involved in. Such collisions are not recorded in the ship's log. The extent of damage was significant:

> *The USS PARTRIDGE was dry-docked from 27 February to 3 March 1944 to repair damage to underwater hull caused by experimental towing alongside.*

The memo lacks details as to what happened aboard the ship to cause the collision and, in fact, what kind of collision occurred at all. The repairs were an unneeded burden and would have raised eyebrows higher in command:

> *On the starboard side of the lower rubbing strake was reinforced from frame 331/2 to frame 51 by spot welded section of half round steel. A patch 18" x 20" was welded over leaks at frame 38 and a 28" x 30" patch was welded over leaks at frames 41 and 42. Lost or leaking rivets were replaced...*

In late March, the *Partridge* was involved in a collision with a motor launch causing significant damaged to the British craft and endangering other craft moored in the harbor. The ship's log records the moment the *Partridge* struck the HMS ML 907 and the domino effect it had in the crowded harbor:

1540 C/s to full astern, c/s to emergency full astern, c/s to stop. Bow struck HMS ML (NR) 907 amid ship at stern. ML 907 at the time moored starboard side to port side of HMS Benbecula, moored at East Branch Docks, Tilbury, Essex, England. ML's mooring lines carried away, allowing ML to become adrift and causing her to collide starboard side of bow to port quarter of USS Cormorant. Moored starboard side to dock, forward of HMS Benbecula.

The damage to the British ship was extensive:

Damage sustained to ML 907 listed as follows; 1. Bollard broken on forecastle, starboard side. 2. Fairlead broken on forecastle, starboard side. 3. Ruffing strake, starboard side damaged. 4. Towing Eye, starboard, forward, broken from base plate. 5. Stanchions damaged starboard forward, 6. Two (2) wire rail nettings damaged starboard side, forward. 7. Brass screws sheered from stern piece. 8. Base plate, for chemical smoke apparatus badly damaged. 9. Rubbing strake on stern section badly damaged.

As an isolated incident, the collision was minor. But throughout the spring, incidents began to accumulate. On April 4, 1944, the *Partridge* was steaming with two vessels in tow. The ship's logs report:

> *Second tow broke loose. Commenced swinging to port. Stopped engines. 0843 Resumed speed at 2.9 knots (30 RPM), steering various course at various speeds, attempting to recover tow. 0922 Abandoned attempt to recover tow.*

The USS *Partridge*, with a stellar record for performance in the Caribbean, was suddenly not up to even the simplest task. Now her duties focused solely on her ability to deliver a tow safely to a destination. Unlike the Caribbean where unexpected opportunities for heroics were needed, in the days immediately before D-Day, the Allies just needed structures for Mulberry to be delivered reliably and on time. Losing a tow altogether was cause for alarm and wouldn't go unnoticed by higher command for long. But there was more to come that would make its flaws in leadership evident to the admiralty.

For the time being, there were no repercussions for Caldin or the *Partridge* for the collision. Caldin's note that the tow was experimental may have been taken into consideration and bought him time, for now. But the damage, nonetheless, had taken a valuable tug out of commission when the Navy needed it most.

During this period my grandfather frequently performed the duty of ferrying Caldin from the ship to shore and back again. Although the captain never discussed details of his shore visits, he often related his displeasure at having to answer to admirals who "sat in an office all day." On return trips, Caldin was often intoxicated and appreciated my grandfather's silence in the matter.

Caldin's habit of harshly punishing his crew for minor infractions while major problems emerged and his run-ins with higher command are the points where the stories of the *Partridge* and the *Caine* merge.

In one of the more famous passages from *The Caine Mutiny*, Queeg ends up losing control of his ship when his attention is diverted by a minor issue. While berating a sailor for his shirt coming untucked, Queeg allows the ship to come in a full circle and cut its tow line. He then makes matters worse by refusing to let the crew rescue the tow, radioing instead into base to ask for instructions.

The incident is recalled later with Captain Grace, who tries to suss out what exactly is going wrong aboard the ship. It's easy to apply the dialogue Queeg has with Grace regarding a mishap at sea to the one Caldin certainly had with his superiors.

> *"Well, hang it, man, first time under way you run up on the mud—of course, that can happen to anybody—but then you try to duck a grounding report and when you do send one in upon request, why, it's just a phony gun deck job. And then what do you call that dispatch to us yesterday? 'Dear me, I've lost a target, please, ComServPac, what shall I do?' Admiral blew up like a land mine. Not because you lost the target—because you couldn't make a decision that was so obvious a seaman 2nd class could have made it! If the function of command isn't to make decisions and take responsibility, what is it?"*

It's clear that Queeg is desperate to succeed, but doesn't have the skills to make sound decisions independently. Like Caldin, Queeg pushed blame both up and down the chain of command. Captain Grace offers him a way out:

> "Commander Queeg, I believe it's possible to transfer you to a stateside assignment—with no reflection whatever, on your performance of duties aboard the Caine. Among other things, as you know, you're rather senior for this post. I understand the squadron is filling up with CO's who are reserve lieutenant commanders and even lieutenants—"

Queeg refuses:

> "And I wonder how that would look in my record, sir—relieved of my first command after one month!"

> "I am the captain of the Caine, and I intend to remain captain, and while I'm captain the Caine will carry out all its assignments or go to the bottom trying."

It's certain that Dayton Clark's command took notice of Caldin's loss of a tow and the small collisions at sea. And it's also certain that Caldin tried to sweep it under the rug. But the failure of a command at this stage of Mulberry wasn't desirable. The command was so swamped with work that correcting a small issue aboard one ship in the flotilla probably didn't even warrant the paperwork. Caldin probably didn't even need to defend his position as ardently as Queeg did in Hawaii.

In the crowded waterways of Britain, it was inevitable that accidents would happen. Caldin was capable of handling the *Partridge* in a technical sense. No man in the U.S. Navy could be promoted as commanding officer if he didn't have some of the skill necessary to guide a ship safely through a harbor. Moreover, he would have been backed by a crew and officers who had the best interests of the ship at heart.

The challenges of Operation Mulberry were not insignificant. But these challenges and the dangers that lay ahead (and for that matter around) the *Partridge,* likely further contributed to the crew's doubt about their leader.

If there was a tipping point aboard the *Partridge,* it came on March 8, 1944. Although Caldin's relationship with his officers and crew had been poor through the full two months of his command, on this date any remaining confidence in him as a commander dissipated. It also marks the date at which his command flaws would no longer go unnoticed by Navy command.

Chapter 11
Standing at the Door

It was a long way from Latrobe.

The thought had drifted through Mike Rich's mind more than once. In basic training. During officers' training. During the rough crossing in this bathtub they called the *Partridge*.

And here he was again. A long way from a life in a Western Pennsylvania town. This time on a train creaking its way into a city that had seen better days: London.

Mike Rich was a middle-class kid. If it weren't for the war, Europe would have remained a thing he would have only seen in newsreels.

And he had seen plenty of newsreels of London. Mostly of the bombing. But nothing could prepare him for the state of a city where almost 30,000 people had died in explosions and fires, or were buried alive under piles of smoldering rubble.

"Jesus. Look at that..." The accent emanating from Rich's companion was as distinct and foreign as the Brits around him. Born out of the harbors of New York City, Cooney's thick Irish-American brogue was layered with years of experience at sea, reaching back into the Great War, when he last saw the city. Now they were both witnessing glimpses of the destruction German bombs had inflicted on the city.

"Just look at that..."

It was a rare moment of reflection for Cooney, who seemed to take the hustle and bustle of the war in stride. The fleets of warships, landing craft, and service boats, the barrage balloons, ACK ACK guns, and the formations of bombers and fighters: none of it mattered much to Joe so much as keeping the lines straight and taut and towing whatever it was that needed to be towed to the right place at the right time.

The train creaked into the station and whatever reflection Cooney allowed himself came to an end. He moved out of his seat and toward the door. Following Cooney out of the train and down the platform, Rich realized that he had never seen the Irishman in his dress uniform. Or anything close to it. He usually saw Cooney on deck directing men on the tow lines, or below deck scratching his head with the engine room mechanic nicknamed Spider. Occasionally he would pop his head onto the bridge- mostly to berate the stupidity of the idiots making decisions there. But just a few days earlier, Joe had cemented himself in the minds of the officers and crew of the *Partridge*. He wasn't just an experienced father-figure. He was someone who took command when they needed him.

The two officers made their way through the crowded London streets, which teamed with a sea of uniforms from just about every branch of the military, and more than a few countries. They found the office at Whitehall where they were to pick up orders and deliver them, unopened, back to the ship. But they were kept waiting in a room outside an admiral's office. Rich had an uneasy feeling that grew exponentially as the clock ticked and the minutes grew into an hour. Finally, they were ushered in. Looking down at a pile of papers, his face almost completely obscured by smoke, the admiral spoke with a cigar clenched in his mouth: "At ease."

Rich expected the rest of the conversation to go somewhat the same way it started. The admiral would probably not even look up at them. Short declarative sentences. Orders. Then dismissed.

But the admiral lifted his head and methodically removed his cigar, relaxing back into his chair as though that small action was a switch that turned on the present moment in time. Two men, from a small ship, playing a small part in a big war, were suddenly in front of him: a tugboat captain and a college kid turned naval officer.

"So boys. Tell me. What in the hell is going on aboard the *Partridge*?"

The admiral wasn't talking about harsh punishments or archaic naval tools. He was talking about the day Joe Cooney saved the ship.

That day was March 8, 1944 and, like on many other days, it started with the *Partridge* towing. The ship, along with the USS *Cormorant,* the HMRNN *Tug Rodevee,* and the HMS *Eagle,* was towing the Phoenix Unit C-130 to Dungeness from Tilbury, where it had been constructed.

One of the smaller caissons, the Phoenix C-130 was still massive. It weighed nearly 2,000 tons and rose over 25 feet out of the water. Still, because it was smaller in size, the *Partridge* was able to make between five and six knots, practically a racing speed by Mulberry standards. At the time, the *Partridge* was towing the Phoenix with 500 feet of tow wire. It was a length specified by Caldin. It was too much. And that decision would have dire results.

Joe Cooney knew immediately that the tow line was too long. The slack was enough to snag on the bottom of the channel. That could cause a whole array of problems - from damaging the towing equipment to snapping the tow line to losing control of both the ship and the Phoenix.

"What the hell are you guys doing? If we let that fucking line out any more, we'll be dredging the fucking channel!"

It was the kind of interruption that would normally be met with some laughs. But on the occasion of this outburst, the atmosphere on the bridge was icy and still. Caldin had already berated other officers for questioning his order to let out the tow and everyone present braced themselves for another outburst. But Lt. Caldin remained calm. Staring over the rims of his glasses out the bridge windows, he addressed Cooney without making eye contact.

"Return to your post, Mr. Cooney." His tone reminded the other officers of a teacher addressing an unruly student. It was a tone easily and often mocked aboard the ship. "We have things well under control up here."

Cooney's eyes darted to the other officers on the bridge. Buffum. Lefavor. Rich. With things under control or not, he knew the score: no one was defying the Captain. The tow line was let out too long, but questioning the captain's orders for a second or third time was out of the question.

It's not clear why Caldin resisted reigning in the tow line. He may have misinterpreted the order that stated the exact length the tow wire was to be or it may have been an arbitrary decision he made in the moment. Or he may have just stuck to a decision more doggedly the more he met resistance.

Cooney slammed the door on the way out. Caldin pursed his lips, calculating whether to pursue punishment for the infraction. He had issued demerits to other officers. Confined some to quarters. He had even stripped them of rank and duty. In fact, he had issued punishments earlier that day to officers who questioned his authority to lock a young sailor in a paint closet below deck for disorderly conduct. After all, the kid, Doyle, was a serial offender and he didn't need a group of officers citing naval code to their captain to mask leniency.

But he had never taken any action toward Cooney. Maybe it was the respect the other men had for the Irishman. Maybe it was his age. Nearly everyone else aboard was half their age. He may have simply looked at everyone younger than Cooney and himself as a boy.

Now that the door to the bridge was shut, an uneasy quiet fell over the cramped space. The helmsman stared straight ahead, keenly aware that the notorious Caldin stood over his shoulder. Tom Buffum stood by, communicating with the engine room. Like Rich, Buffum had few plans to continue in the Navy. He had been aboard the ship a little bit longer than Rich and seemed to bond well with the men, with his friendly personality and pleasant singing voice.

But the inexperience of Rich and Buffum and Cooney's ignorance of naval protocol was more than offset by Lt. Frank Lefavor. Lefavor, the ship's executive officer (XO), was a broad-shouldered, imposing figure at over 6 foot 3 who had been with the ship since the Caribbean tour and served along with Jim White. Frank had joined the Navy in '32 and worked his way up to officer status. He knew the pivotal role a working ship like the *Partridge* was playing now was a rare moment in history and just as rare a career opportunity. But it was all going terribly wrong.

As the captain's right-hand man, Lefavor should have been his eyes and ears aboard the ship. Instead, he spent much of his time avoiding Caldin; even ducking into storage closets when they were about to pass in the narrow passageways of the ship. An encounter with Caldin, no matter how minor, was likely to end in conflict. Lefavor had been removed as XO twice, only to be reinstated, but the damage to his Navy career may have already been done. The captain was as fickle about lifting punishments as he was about giving them out. Even worse, these actions undermined Lefavor's ability to be an effective XO.

The stony silence on the bridge stood in stark contrast to the rest of the ship. Outside, engines roared and the wind blew hard against the voices of men working the lines. The relative silence on the bridge made it almost easy to forget about the huge structure behind the tiny ship.

The Phoenix looked distinctly un-nautical trailing behind the ship. It was a large concrete rectangle and it was immense. Twenty-five feet high and as long as a city block, it dwarfed the *Partridge* that strained to keep a few knots under way.

"Mr. Lefavor, tell the men to let out the line another 50."

Lefavor tensed. It was classic Caldin. In his world and on his ship, two wrongs made a right. If Cooney wanted the line shortened, Caldin would give the order to lengthen it. Lefavor had read the order. He knew Caldin had read it. The line was to be kept tight and the Mulberry close.

But Caldin was the captain of a ship in the U.S. Navy and his word was that of God. He had worked up from saloon owner's son to the commander of a vessel engaged in one of the greatest naval missions of all time.

Paranoid, vindictive, and incompetent: Lefavor had always thought Caldin's personality was a dangerous combination and now everyone aboard the *Partridge* would witness how. The massive Mulberry could crush a vessel like the *Partridge*. Getting farther away from it could snag the tow line. But on this deck, on this rusty hull, it was Caldin's Navy, the only one that mattered.

Was he running away from the hulking tow? Everyone had joked about it. At five knots, they were an easy target for the German E-boats or subs. And the giant concrete block didn't do much for their low profile in the water or from the air. But did Caldin really think he was outrunning that kind of danger?

"Lieutenant? Is there a problem?"

Lefavor bristled at the reference. He shared the same rank as the captain, yet Caldin used every opportunity to demonstrate his absolute authority. Lefavor had seen his type before. Give a guy a little bit of authority and suddenly he's a king. *Paranoid, vindictive, and incompetent*. Lefavor mulled the words again. They fit—but there was something else, too. Something unstable about the man. He braved a response:

"Captain, we're already twice as far out as the order states."

"Mr. Lefavor, does that order know the conditions of the sea or the state of the craft or her crew? Does the order state that we are to follow blindly a list of numbers or follow the judgment of a captain with 25 years of experience at sea?"

Lefavor braced himself. Another demotion. Docking pay. Confined to cabin. Maybe he'd just put himself out of misery with a court martial.

But Caldin's building tirade was cut short.

At 8:31 AM, Joe Cooney's prediction came true. The Phoenix unit's tow wire became snagged on the bottom of the channel. The two ends of the cable moved toward each other like the ends of scissors on a hinge, sending the *Partridge* and the Phoenix on a collision course.

The ship shook and rattled as the diesel engines roared beneath the bridge. Smoke billowed out of the stack. But the ship never increased its speed through the water. Worse still, she was still drifting to starboard.

Mike Rich looked out toward the Phoenix and was stunned by what he saw. It was no longer behind the ship, but drifting directly toward it. It towered over the small boat like a drifting apartment block. It was the inevitable slow motion of a collision at sea, where large bodies moved out of control based on decisions made three or four steps prior. In all of the confusion, one thing was certain: the ship was roaring at full speed and the Phoenix loomed closer to their starboard side. The *Partridge* was going to collide with an object much larger than itself and moving with greater momentum.

The bridge door swung open. It was Joe Cooney.

"Goddamn it! We need to drop the line and move full reverse."

The silent world of the bridge seemed to snap. Lefavor shot his eyes to Buffum then to Caldin.

"Captain. Full reverse?"

Caldin did not respond. The helmsman eyed Lefavor nervously. Caldin pursed his lips and began breathing out of his nose. Lefavor blurted it out:

"Sailor, full reverse. Mr. Cooney, tell the men to cut the line."

"Sailor, ignore that order!" Caldin pushed up his glasses and stared intensely as though the order came from someone else.

"Full stop," ordered Caldin.

The order echoed through the helmsman to the engine room and the engine fell silent. In the silence, the line groaned while the Mulberry unit loomed overhead. The helmsmen looked about helplessly to Lefavor then to Rich. They both turned their eyes to Caldin, who maintained the long stare broken only by another push of his spectacles.

Cooney stepped in and stood close to Lefavor. Almost whispering, he reiterated the point.

"We need to full reverse and cut that line. This thing's going to hit."

"Helmsman, the order stands. Engines full stop." The order emanated from the sweaty little man who stood in command. All the months of petty drills, punishments, investigations; it all came down to this moment of critical action.

"He doesn't want to look at it," thought Lefavor. "He doesn't want to see when it hits."

And when it came, it was a long, slow, sickening groan of metal torn apart deep in the belly of the ship.

The sound was a reminder of the very thin and fragile skin that kept this world intact above the water line. It was a horrific low chorus that continued on for some time followed by a silence—as though the collective ears of the ship were waiting for some sign that the ship would float or sink. But then there were screaming men, flooded compartments, hull breaches, and the ship listing to the port side. She was going down.

History is littered with leaders who exhibit poor decision-making due to excessive pride. And there are more than a few leaders who are purely incompetent. But what happened next places Adnah Caldin's leadership in a category of its own.

In this moment of crisis, Caldin stood completely and utterly paralyzed. It may have been the shock of the collision or the cumulative impact of the previous collisions. The incident may have taken him back to his experience aboard the *Auk*, when the compartments of that ship flooded with water during a storm off the coast of Cape Cod.

Whatever the case, at this moment of extreme crisis, the kind of moment that defines a captain's command, Caldin did the unthinkable.

"He just left the bridge," recalled Mike Rich. "He just left without saying a word and locked himself in his cabin."

It was a stunning, unbelievable act. Caldin's actions so far had been arrogant and unreasonable. But leaving the bridge while the ship was heavily damaged seemed insane. Decades later, the men who were on the bridge and witnessed Caldin's flight were still baffled by his actions. It was the greatest betrayal of a crew's trust in their captain.

No one remembers Joe Cooney taking charge. They just remember him saving the ship. He ordered the ship maneuvered to the port and then to the starboard and to the port again, unsnagged the tow wire and gained control of the ship and the tow.

But there was another problem. With water rising below deck, and the ship's ability to stay afloat in question, Charlie Doyle was still below deck, locked in a paint closet.

"I don't know what the kid did," recalled Joe Shannon. "He was always getting in trouble with Caldin. Who knows what it was this time."

As a group struggled to try to break in the door to save Doyle, the rest of the crew was working to save the ship, but she was badly damaged. The punched hole was flooding compartments throughout the ship—as much as 14 feet in some. Cooney ordered the crew to affix temporary patches on the hull and operate pumps to keep the water levels from rising. It was all routine and by the book, but it was accomplished without a captain on the bridge.

A British trawler was called on for assistance and took on the weight of the Phoenix. By 9:32 the situation was under control, the ship stable, and Doyle freed from the closet.

With the assistance of other ships, the *Partridge* limped to harbor. The crisis had passed. On any other ship in any other situation, the feeling would have been relief that the ship had passed out of harm's way. But for the crew and officers on the bridge, a peculiar sensation passed over them. Their captain had abandoned them on the bridge at a crisis point. Caldin had certainly been hard on the crew, but everyone had a story to tell about an asshole of a captain they had once served under.

But this was an act of instability, abandonment, and, worst of all, cowardice. Even Caldin's poor judgement in locking a member of the crew below deck while underway could be accounted for due to his argumentative personality. But fleeing the bridge shook the officer's and crew's confidence to the core.

Something seemed to break that day. In addition to the ship being crippled, the morale aboard cracked. Caldin reacted by dishing out punishments more frequently. On March 11 he reduced the rank of two men and on March 14 he relieved Frank Lefavor of duty as executive commander, confining him to quarters indefinitely. The order was modified later that same day stating that "confinement of Lt (jg) F. A. Lefavor modified to suspension from duty for a period of 10 days." In the log, this statement is followed by another: "Ship resting on blocks."

The officers aboard the *Partridge* were now seriously concerned about Caldin's leadership and its impact on their lives and the lives of the crew. In the past they may have disagreed with his tactics or have disliked his demeanor. Now not only had he made a serious miscalculation that put the ship in danger, but he fled his command at a crucial moment that put the safety of the men aboard in jeopardy. Worse still, his blatant disregard for Navy regulations put at least one crew member, Charlie Doyle, in mortal danger.

There was talk of going above Caldin to command. But many, including Frank Lefavor, thought this was impossible. Superior officers wouldn't take the complaints of an engineering officer turned XO seriously and, worse still, Caldin would be informed of their complaint. There would be more punishments. More reductions in rank and pay. More arcane rules. More misery.

But tension was growing. The ship would be sailing into combat soon. There were constant reminders that they were on an active front in the war. Air raids sounded daily in Tilbury, Portsmouth, and Selsey Bill, all ports the *Partridge* frequented. The Germans were privy to something going on leading up to an invasion and were particularly targeting the elements of Mulberry. Nightly bombardment, as well as the terrifying slow tow up the British coast after the collision, were only a preamble to what all the men knew was coming during the invasion.

Some of the officers had an ace up their sleeve, however. A way to communicate up the chain of command without putting their career in danger. Several of the officers, including Tom Buffum, were members of the Masons, which was a fairly common occurrence in the Navy. This would allow the officers to speak in confidence, Mason to Mason, to another officer without fear of word spreading up and down the chain of command. This conversation could at least raise the possibility of an investigation without a formal complaint from any of the sailors and officers aboard the *Partridge.* And it would save them from any repercussions from Caldin and wouldn't mar their record. There weren't any promises, but the question could be raised.

For his part, Mike Rich said that, originally, the trip was planned solely to collect plans on the coming invasion. Reporting Caldin to his superior officers was an accident of time and place.

"As far as I was concerned, CWO Cooney and I were in London to receive the plans for our part in Operation Mulberry," recalled Rich decades later.

But the communication could have happened with or without the knowledge of Joe Cooney or Mike Rich. In fact, it would be better for all involved if they didn't know. The quiet conversation secured a promise that, at the very least, the question would be raised. And it was all that the men of the *Partridge* could ask.

In March 1944, Joe Cooney and Mike Rich made their trip to the Navy's admiralty officer at Whitehall Place in the heart of London. It's a day that remained fixed in the hearts and minds of the sailors aboard the ship for decades to come. It was the day that Cooney and Rich went above Caldin's head and fixed the problem

Standing in London, in an admiral's office, Rich realized the true reason for the trip. Cooney wasn't here to fetch some orders. He was the only man aboard that could dare cross the line into what some would call mutiny.

"What the hell is going on aboard the *Partridge*?"

If there was a man to answer that question, it certainly wouldn't be Rich, a kid fresh from officer's training. Or Lefavor, the man with a career in the Navy ahead of him. Or Buffum, the Ivy League grad. It would be the Irish tugboat captain who kept the *Partridge* afloat in her hour of need that would stick out his neck to tell their story. His age carried weight with younger officers who significantly outranked him. Also, his experience on tugboats in the busiest harbor in the world was held in high regard among those commanding Mulberry.

Even after answering that question truthfully, and risking insubordination, both Cooney and Rich thought that little or nothing would come of it. Finding a sympathetic ear in the midst of planning for one of the largest military operations in history was more than they could hope for. This was the command of Dayton Clark whose personality didn't lend itself to sympathy or patience.

It seemed likely that two junior officers laying out the problems aboard their ship would have been, at best, told to pack it back to their ship, keep their noses to the grindstone, and stop bothering higher command about their problems.

"We assumed that after we told him the situation aboard that would be the end of it," said Mike Rich decades later.

Maybe it was because of a secret conversation whispered between two Masons. Or maybe it was because Moran's tugs were in short supply. Or maybe the upcoming mission was so critical. Whatever the reason, it was not, as Rich predicted, the end of it.

Word traveled through the chain of command and, within days, the Commander Landing Craft and Bases launched a formal investigation into conditions aboard the USS *Partridge*.

Ensign Mike Rich whose trip to London with Joe Cooney brought conditions aboard the Partridge to the attention of the Navy admiralty

Chapter 12
Lt. Commander Janeway's Investigation

On April 23, 1944, at noon, Lt. Commander E. G. Janeway stepped aboard the USS *Partridge*. He carried a confidential letter from the Commander Landing Craft and Bases naming him as the sole member on a board of investigation regarding the conditions on the aging minesweeper.

Janeway's arrival was shocking to the officers and crew of the *Partridge*. Why was someone from Command interested in this old bath tub now?

Entering the world of the *Partridge,* Janeway was both a witness and participant in the tension that existed between the regular Navy and reservists. He was serving his country during wartime, but had enjoyed a privileged life before the war. He was an amateur yachtsman and Wall Street broker, and came from a moneyed family with an estate on Long Island. Adnah Caldin had served nearly 25 years in the Navy and yet had only achieved the rank of chief warrant officer, being handed a temporary rank of lieutenant when war broke out. Janeway had entered the Navy in the reserves as a Lt. Commander, instantly outranking Caldin. Yet he was here to pass judgement on a man who had served his country most of his adult life.

But all of the social injustice of the past and present didn't matter now. Janeway was there to listen and learn and find out how so much could go so wrong. The *Partridge* was just a small part of Mulberry, but for the operation to succeed almost everything had to go right. Almost everything aboard this ship was going wrong. Lieutenant Commander Janeway was aboard to find out why. And if the "90-day wonders," reserve officers, and recently drafted sailors made for a better, more effective ship for the upcoming invasion, then Adnah Caldin would have to pay the price.

Janeway's orders gave him the authority to investigate conditions aboard and assess whether Lieutenant Caldin was fit to command the *Partridge* or any vessel in the United States Navy. His unannounced arrival put Caldin in the awkward position of ingratiating himself to a higher authority, welcoming him aboard, and offering him precious space to work in, all the time knowing that the Lieutenant Commander was there to question what he valued more than anything: command.

As Janeway set up the investigation, word quietly spread. Some crewmembers may have noted the arrival of some strange Navy brass, but his arrival sent a shockwave through the officers. Mike Rich was astonished. Had his meeting in London really sparked this? And what exactly had he sparked? From where he stood, he and Cooney might very well be hauled off and tried for mutiny after this well-heeled lieutenant commander headed back to London.

Rich was an ensign fresh out of training. The epitome of the "90-day wonder." A little over a year ago he was a kid in college back in Pennsylvania. Now he was in the middle of a war zone on the eve of one of the great naval operations of all time, and he had somehow brought the focus of higher naval authority down on the *Partridge* and her commander. A Lt. Commander acting under the higher authority of Commander, Landing Craft and Bases (ComLanCrab), had set up an interview room aboard the ship.

For a naval officer, and in fact any military officer, there is a responsibility to obey orders from a superior officer and to abide by the code of that branch of the military. The Navy is both direct and confusing in this regard. The Navy Code is explicit in every detail of life aboard a ship. Everything from food supplies to crew punishments to navigation are dictated by the captain. At the same time, however, the code is adamant about the authority of a captain aboard a ship. The regulations have an inherent contradiction. Are Navy officers beholden to the regulations or to their captain? Were the conditions aboard the *Partridge* as much the fault of its officers as they were Caldin's? Could they or should they have done everything they could to report any violations to higher authorities? Or would that, itself, have been a violation of Navy code?

Janeway was aboard to find out. He began with the officers.

Lt. Commander Janeway was different than most men aboard the ship. They were kids from farms or small towns. The majority were just out of school. Some had young families, and most came from modest means. They were young men who had their entire lives ahead of them and who looked at the war as a great adventure. Janeway's privileged background was another strata that made up the U.S. military during the war.

His father, Dr. Edward Janeway, had been a prominent physician at the turn of the century. Janeway struggled early in his career, finding work in a metal shop after dropping out of Yale. But he soon found his way onto Wall Street and enjoyed many privileges of being born into and marrying into well-connected families.

Janeway exemplified the kind of citizen that Wouk wrote about in *The Caine Mutiny*—well educated, ambitious, and capable. In the late 1930s, Janeway was leading a comfortable life raising a family and advancing his career. He and his wife Elinor enjoyed summers in Maine on a private island and traveled widely.

Like Joe Cooney, he was somewhat advanced in years to have joined the military. A father of five children back in Long Island, Janeway was well into his forties when the Navy accepted him. After initial training, he was assigned to command an LST maintenance base in Deptford, U.K., far from the combat ship assignment he hoped for.

But if Janeway had sought adventure in the middle years of his life, he found a Navy in need of organization, leadership, and direction. More often than not, problems were caused by too little discipline, too much freedom, and crews that were young and inexperienced. He may have joined the Navy to see the world, but instead, he saw bureaucratic problems in need of solutions.

He was sent aboard the *Partridge* to determine the cause of her poor performance and also to verify what Cooney and Rich had conveyed to Navy brass. He had expected to return a list of recommendations based on a more balanced view of what Cooney and Rich conveyed.

Instead, Janeway's investigation was about to undo the God-like power the Navy bestowed on a ship's captain.

Janeway was surprised to have been asked to conduct this investigation. It was not uncommon for the men aboard a small ship like this to vilify an unlikeable captain, but the Navy seldom took any kind of action. Whatever logic brought him here, Janeway wasn't aboard the *Partridge* to determine how "likeable" Caldin was. He was there to find out why so much had gone wrong during the short time Caldin had the ship in his command. He had seen plenty of nervous, martinet types like Caldin. They were desperate to assert their authority and had just enough ambition to get themselves in trouble. He thought that, at worst, Caldin would be assigned to another ship and some of the senior officers would be reprimanded.

But interviews with Rich, Lefavor, Buffum, and Cooney revealed a situation aboard the *Partridge* that was quickly unravelling. These officers weren't challenging their Captain's authority; they were protecting their ship and the men aboard.

In most of the cases, the officers themselves were punished for trying to protect the men under them. At times Caldin was violating Navy code placing his men in grave danger.

And to hear these officers verify each other's stories independently was remarkable. While sailors might view life aboard ship as filled with unfair punishments and egregious violations of their own liberty, officers had their own command issues to deal with. In a perfect command situation, the authority of a captain would be backed up their own authority.

But in his interviews, Janeway found the opposite to be true. Officers found it difficult to enforce Caldin's authority because his orders were often impossible to carry out against Navy regulations. To make matters worse, the captain often unfairly reprimanded sailors who were under the direct command of his senior officers.

And then there was the matter of the *Phoenix* unit collision. Ships had collided with objects through no fault of their commanding officers. And often captains who did make mistakes would be covered by their crew, either out of a sense of duty or an appreciation for the man who carried the weight of command for the entire ship. But Caldin fled the bridge, a detail noted by all officers aboard.

What was emerging was not a group of officers sniping at their superior officer, but a group of men trying their best to uphold the tenet that the Captain's word is final while preserving the survival of the ship. More experienced officers might have felt it perfectly within their rights to report Caldin's behavior, but the officers aboard the *Partridge* were paralyzed. The executive officer Frank Lefavor had a strong desire to perform the duties of a line officer, but was bewildered at Caldin's actions and left powerless to do anything about it. The collision seemed to be the breaking point for most officers.

After interviewing the *Partridge's* officers, Janeway decided to expand his investigation. By the time the investigation was over, Janeway had interviewed every man aboard the ship, some extensively. Nearly a quarter of them had received some kind of reduction in rank and all had stories that echoed their officer's claims. Many of the men had been aboard the ship for years and had served under S.E. Kenney and Snipes with distinguished records—many of these same men now found themselves lower in rank and with less pay than when they had begun in the Navy.

And Caldin's fury seemed to grow the more the crew was under pressure. Men related stories to Janeway of Caldin shouting insults at men through a megaphone while a bombardon, a cross-shaped floating breakwater, was towed by the *Partridge*. Others have him writing up the engine room crew after his command caused a collision at Portsmouth. The ship's logs show that days after the ship struck the Phoenix C-130, Caldin demoted more than a half dozen men in a single day.

Janeway's interview captured the gambit of personalities aboard the ship from the wise-cracking Donald Wampler to the capable and confident Bill Ames to men like my grandfather, whose duties included transporting an isolated and often intoxicated Caldin back and forth to shore in a whale boat. Each had a story that wove a larger narrative for Janeway that ran counter to an old adage from the time men first took to the sea: the captain's word is final.

Perhaps it was time to question that adage. After all, the world was at war, and the *Partridge's* small role in the coming invasion was vital to the overall effort. In a modern, mechanized war, there was little room for personality-driven command style. In this context, the captain was really more of a manager with limited authority.

On the other hand, war or no war, the sanctity of the Captain was rarely questioned. Strict adherence to the chain of command was and still is deeply ingrained in the military.

Joseph Conrad's rumination on the role of the captain is often cited in decommissioning ceremonies and as an overall creed of the U.S. Navy and Navies all over the world:

> *"A ship at sea is a different world unto herself and in consideration of the protracted and distant operations of the fleet units, the Navy must place great power, responsibility and trust in the hands of those leaders chosen for command."*

> *"In each ship, there is one man who, in the hour of emergency or peril at sea, can turn to no other man. There is one man alone who is ultimately responsible for the safe navigation, engineering performance, accurate gunfire, and morale of his ship. He is the Commanding Officer. He is the ship..."*

It's not easy to dismantle any structure of leadership, but removing a captain from command calls into question someone who is supposed to be unquestionable. Even on the *Partridge,* the command was sacrosanct because if the captain's absolute authority is questioned somewhere it is questioned everywhere. It is a code held not just in the U.S. Navy, but in ships throughout the world.

These were the major considerations for Janeway during his investigation. According to Mike Rich,

Janeway was very concerned about the morale aboard the ship—it was the main focus of the investigation.

At some point during the questioning, a sailor had to be confined for drunken and disorderly conduct. It was an ominous sign. Janeway seemed to shift his investigation away from seeking blame to seeking a solution to an obvious problem. If the *Partridge* was to function as a part of Operation Mulberry then her command would have to change.

There was no drama. No major courtroom confrontation. No accusations in front of a public audience. Only Janeway's notes taken in pencil on a simple pad of paper and a recommendation.

A communication from the Commander, Landing Craft and Bases (COMLANCRAB), Eleventh Amphibious Force to the Chief of Naval Personnel, summarizes Janeway's report and the conclusions the Navy made:

> *That such conditions could be allowed to exist on any ship of the U.S. Navy can only partially be condoned by (1) the type of duty the ship has been in this theatre with little or no opportunity for responsible seniors to observe the conditions aboard, and (2) the inexperience of the junior officers resulting in lack of knowledge as to how to inform the proper seniors at an earlier date of these conditions.*

An outgoing dispatch from Commander Navy Europe (ComNavEU) is less kind. Not only is Caldin irresponsible and unfit to command the *Partridge,* he is, according to the dispatch, a detriment to the entire naval operation in Europe:

REQUEST IMMEDIATE RETURN OF LT A N CALDIN USN TO US FOR SUCH ACTION BUPERS (Bureau of Personnel) DESIRE TO TAKE IN HIS CASE. IT WAS NECESSARY TO RELIEVE HIM OF HIS COMMAND USS PARTRIDGE DUE TO COMPLETE LACK LEADERSHIP, SHIP CONTROL, AND JUDGEMENT REQUIRED OF COMMANDING OFFICER. STUDY OF REPORT OF INVESTIGATION CASTS GRAVE DOUBTS OF HIS FITNESS AS COMMISSIONED OFFICER AND REVOCATION HIS COMMISSION WILL BE RECOMMENDED IN FORWARDING ENDORSEMENT. HIS RETENTION TO THIS COMMAND IN ANY CAPACITY CONSIDERED DETRIMENT TO BEST INTEREST NAVAL FORCES EUROPE. HE IS NOW ATTACHED USNAAB NORE AWAITING ASSIGNMENT. COMPLETE REPORT BEING FORWARDED.

But the "complete report" is not attached to these dispatches. As of this writing, it still has not been found. Yet the conclusions the dispatches carry out give us clues into what the report revealed.

Caldin wasn't the only officer aboard referenced in Janeway's report. Frank Lefavor, the executive officer, also was mentioned. Lefavor had been a highly regarded Chief Engineer but had ambitions to move up as a line officer. Lefavor did this and more by achieving the position of executive officer aboard the *Partridge*.

Even though Lefavor and Caldin had clashed many times aboard the *Partridge* and he had tried to act as a counterweight to Caldin's command, the Navy saw the conditions aboard the ship to be, at least in a small part, his responsibility, mainly because he didn't report conditions to a higher authority. The report makes reference to the "*inexperience of the junior officer resulting in lack of knowledge as to how to inform the proper seniors at an earlier date of these conditions.*"

"There was no way that we could have gone above his head," remarked Mike Rich after seeing these dispatches almost 65 years after they were sent. He was echoing the feelings of the *Caine's* Steve Maryk and Tom Keefer moments before they enter a meeting with Halsey on the *New Jersey*, to discuss Queeg's instability. It's almost possible to imagine a conversation like this between Lefavor and Tom Buffum:

> "*Can't you feel the difference between the New Jersey and the Caine? This is the Navy, here, the real Navy. Our ship is a floating booby hatch...It won't stick, Steve. We haven't got enough on him. When this damn war is over I'm going to be a scribbler again, same as before. But you want to stay in the Navy, don't you? You'll smash yourself, Steve, against a stone wall. You'll be finished in the Navy forever. And Queeg will go right on commanding the Caine—*"

Lefavor, who had dragged himself up as an engineering officer to the bridge, in part by extensively drilling in navigation with Bill Ames, had tried to protect his men against Caldin and paid a price. He ultimately shared the blame with Caldin for conditions aboard the *Partridge*. It isn't certain what would have happened if Lefavor had filed a report against Caldin earlier.

For that matter, it isn't clear in *Caine* what would have happened if Maryk and Keefer had taken a meeting with Halsey. But the perception from the junior officers was consistent. Such a report would have met with deaf ears at best and, at worst, impacted the careers of the regular Navy officers who looked forward to a working lifetime on the seas. Lefavor, Buffum, and Rich may have taken blame from the Navy on this minor report, but they would remain officers in the Navy with their future career opportunities intact. Only Lefavor would pay a price:

> *Lt. (jg) Lefavor is being transferred by dispatch. This officer apparently is a capable engineer but a poor executive. His services will be utilized in his specialty.*

The dispatch goes on to leave the fate of Lt. Caldin up to the Bureau of Personnel. Referring to the full report, COMLANCRAB provided the following recommendations:

> *(F) Due to the urgency of preparation of all forces of this command for combat operations, it is not feasible to try Lieut. A.N. Caldin by general court-martial, and it is recommended that his commission be revoked. This procedure may possibly save an otherwise capable enlisted man for the navy who is most definitely not of the proper officer caliber.*

The above paragraph may contain a silver lining in that Caldin could continue to serve his country in a capacity that was sorely needed. But his career, his hope for advancement, his longing to be a commanding officer in the U.S. Navy during an historic operation—what would turn out to be one of the largest Naval engagements of all time—all that was gone now.

Some remember Caldin departing that day from the ship. Others remember a few days passing before a military escort appeared and led the Captain away from the ship. The ship's log indicates only that he was relieved from command on April 28, some five days after the investigation. However, it is entirely possible that Caldin was led ashore so that contact with the crew was kept to a minimum. He was shipped back to the States and had a hearing before the Bureau of Naval Personnel on June 8, 1944. On June 12 his rank was reverted to his permanent rank of Chief Boatswain, USN. He would never command men at sea again.

On board the *Partridge,* ranks were changing as well. All ranks that had been reduced during Caldin's command were restored as were pay rates. Many of the men affected were simple sailors whose promotion meant more money for them to send home or spend at port. Reducing pay by as little as $20 was the equivalent of over $230 in today's money.

"For the guys, this was a big deal," recalled Ames. "Some of them had wives and family back home so losing that money really hurt. The whole ship was glad to be rid of Caldin, but we were just so surprised that the Navy would just give back those ranks."

The impact on morale was instant. A euphoria swept over the ship and versions of the story began to evolve based on hard facts, soft truths, and conjecture. Cooney and Rich had gone to London under the auspices of getting plans but with a secret agenda. Maybe it was true and maybe it was half true, but it solidified in sailors' minds.

If Joe Cooney had been a father figure before, now he became the protector of the ship. If he had "looked after" the ship on previous occasions, now he looked after the men as well. He had saved the ship when she was in danger of sinking and now he saved the ship from its own captain.

The tough Irishmen who drank rum and coke and homemade whiskey with his men—a working man and father back home—could do no wrong in the eyes of his shipmates. Sailing into the most dangerous waters any of them had ever entered, it seemed that Joe could always save the ship from harm.

Chapter 13
The *Owl* and Captain White

In *The Caine Mutiny,* Wouk records the change in command after Queeg is relieved of duty. Maryk commands the ship on one final mission before returning to Pearl Harbor, still retaining the charisma from his bold endeavor to save the ship from Queeg. But Captain Jim White restored stability to the small minesweeper. Wouk's White not only cooly and professionally brings working order back to the men of *Caine,* he restores faith in the establishment:

The magic had begun to dim in Pearl Harbor with the arrival of Captain White, a good-looking, bright lieutenant of the regular Navy, obviously a troubleshooter. Maryk had shrunk in a day to a subservient dull exec. The adventurous excitement in the wardroom had subsided. All the officers had begun talking humbly again, and guarding their words. White was arid cool and efficient. He acted as though the relief of Queeg had never occurred. He handled the ship as well as Maryk from the first, and he attracted the immediate loyalty of the crew. Willie's vision of the mutiny as a triumph of Reserve heroism over neurotic Academy stupidity languished. The Academy was back in charge, and master of the situation.

This was Wouk's Jim White. Another Jim White had once sat on a folding chair perched on the aft deck of the *Partridge* for his first haircut at sea. Now he sat in a British pub having a round with the officers from the *Owl*. They were drinking to his promotion, a trip back to the States for additional training, and command of a larger, more modern ship presumably in the Pacific. They even joked that they would probably give him a battleship or a cruiser. But behind all the jokes, every man at the table, even aboard the entire *Owl*, would have followed Jim White anywhere. They had been through a lot together. Before the promotion, the drinks, the departure back home, Jim White was a brand new lieutenant commanding his first U.S. Navy vessel on the open ocean in winter in the North Atlantic. It turned out that the rough crossing would be the easier part of the trip.

Trailing behind the *Partridge*, the *Owl* laid anchor in Horta Bay, Fayal in the Azores, February 1944. The Portuguese island had remained neutral throughout the war, but now was openly assisting Allied ships in passage across the Atlantic. On 16 February a group of nine sailors from the *Owl* embarked on a time-honored tradition for sailors confined to ships for long periods at sea. They jumped ship and went ashore for some fun.

Using "Bum Boats" (small boats that pulled alongside Navy and merchant vessels to sell food, souvenirs, and supplies), the nine made it to town and promptly became entangled in a brawl with a group of British sailors. Soon, two Portuguese sailors were drawn into the fighting, followed by a much larger group of their comrades. Seeing they were outnumbered, the *Owl* sailors fled the scene and made their way back to their ship. Near the harbor, the group met two Portuguese soldiers who had not been in the previous tangle. Part of the group passed the soldiers without incident. But when one of the Portuguese soldiers elbowed a sailor named Stanley Marsh things quickly escalated.

Maybe his adrenaline was still high from the previous fighting. Maybe he was frustrated at fleeing the barroom brawl. Maybe he wanted to exact a misplaced revenge for some wrongdoing from the fight. We'll probably never know the reasons why Marsh drew his Navy-issued knife that evening and plunged it deep into the heart of the Portuguese soldier who bumped into him, but that is exactly what he did.

The soldier fell to the ground, dead instantly. Marsh continued the attack, jabbing a second soldier in the arm. Marsh then placed the bloody knife into its sheath and fled the scene.

Four of the *Owl* sailors who had been trailing Marsh came across the dead and wounded soldiers, unaware of what had happened. Helping the wounded soldier to a café, the group determined that the injury needed medical attention and placed the soldier in a taxicab. Those four then voluntarily reported to a police station, where they joined five of their fellow sailors, including Marsh, already apprehended.

The incident was a sudden and stark reminder to Jim White of the challenges of naval command. At 27 years old, White was responsible for a vessel at sea sailing into a major battleground of the largest conflict the world had ever seen. But he was also in charge of a group of unpredictable young men living in close quarters farther from home than any had ever been. Now a group of men under his command had caused an international incident in a neutral port at a time of war.

In a fictionalized version of the *Owl* incident, White would have headed up an investigation revealing the motives behind the murder, perhaps with a twist that would exonerate the innocent and reveal the guilty.

Instead, the incident is pure Jim White. He was characteristically calm under pressure and approached the incident with no drama, no ego. He engaged the Azores most reputable defense attorney, Dr. Antonio Xavier De Mesquita, to defend the nine sailors held in custody, including Marsh. The men were interviewed and all agreed that Marsh was responsible for the stabbings. Marsh denied not only stabbing the two soldiers but of carrying a knife. A diver was employed to search the harbor and Marsh's bunk was turned upside down. No murder weapon was found, but after the surviving soldier positively identified Marsh from his hospital bed, Marsh gave a full confession. He could not give a reason for the stabbings and was sentenced to 25 years in prison. Marsh ended up dying in prison on the island in 1948 of Pott's disease, a form of tuberculosis that affects the spine.

Jim White ended up tightening security aboard the *Owl,* improving lighting on the side of the ship, and forbidding local vessels from coming close to the *Owl.* He also conducted captain's masts, which ended in the court-martial of the men who jumped ship that evening.

For all this drama, White's account is thorough, efficient, and fair. The *Owl* remained on schedule in her journey to Great Britain. White didn't offer leniency or diminish the seriousness of the crime. But he did provide a steady hand of leadership, deferring to higher authorities when the time was right. He called upon U.S. Navy Resources available in the port and worked with them as well as local police and military to ensure that there was justice for the crime.

Perhaps most importantly, he didn't alienate his own officers, but worked with them to help manage the situation. One could see the steady hand of Captain Snipes as an influence on White remaining calm and fair, doling out punishment, but moving on with the mission.

The incident in the Azores tested White's leadership in ways he could have scarcely imagined when he assumed command of the ship in Norfolk. Aboard the *Partridge,* there had been run-ins with local governments, most notably in Cuba, when the ship entered a bay without permission while dodging a submarine. But the Azores presented a gateway into the world in which the *Owl* and the *Partridge* were sailing.

Ports were crowded with sailors and soldiers on leave not only from the massive U.S. Military buildup but from Britain and dozens of other Allied nations. A distinct swagger in the step of many Yanks was duly noted by many British and Canadian soldiers and sailors weary after five years of war. Higher pay in the U.S. military and a habit of wooing British women did little to relieve tensions ashore.

Jim White's experience in the Azores previewed the challenges of command ahead. For the captain of a Bird Boat sailing into Britain in 1944 to take part in Operation Mulberry, the challenges of command wouldn't be confronting the Germans at sea, improvising tactics to save sinking ships, and employing cavalier tactics outside the scope of the small ships duties. The challenges would be in maintaining discipline.

At this stage of the war, the *Owl* and her crew would be confronted with complex and even experimental naval maneuvers that required the full concentration of the crew. Any captain of a small vessel in that theater had to balance these new adversities with discipline that would grant the crew enough freedom to blow off steam but also ensure that they didn't become entangled in onshore scuffles and run-ins with the law.

It's possible to look at the *Owl* incident in two ways. The first is where Jim White's cool and systematic handling of an unfortunate event prevented any deviation from the ship's overall mission in Britain. And the other where poor discipline allowed nine sailors to jump ship and wreak havoc ashore.

It's easy to imagine how Adnah Caldin might have handled a similar event. Much less serious infractions were handled with harsher punishments aboard the *Partridge* before and after the Azores murder. Caldin also tended to blame his fellow officers for perceived shortcomings rather than employ them to solve problems with the crew.

Caldin and White experienced similar challenges in the Azores. As the first port of call after a harrowing cross-Atlantic journey, men indulged heavily in the local drink of choice, cognac. Drunkenness and fighting were not uncommon in the Azores. A tale of murder, however, would have stood out and Caldin would have been among the first to hear about it.

The incident added to the narrative of his command after the Azores. Caldin's upbringing in his father's tavern armed him with an intimate knowledge of how drink and rowdiness could transform men for the worse.

The murder would have strengthened his resolve to have more discipline among sailors and deepened his distrust for the "90-day wonders" who surrounded him in the ranks of officers. With years of Navy training under his belt, and a stiffened resolve to run a tight ship, Caldin would avoid these types of incidents and emerge the successful naval officer he had dreamed of becoming.

Yet, the opposite came to be. White, a young man barely older than many of the youngest sailors aboard the ship, with little Navy training, went through one of the most difficult command situations imaginable and emerged as a confident, fair leader.

Morale aboard a ship is essential. Cramped quarters, extreme conditions, isolation, and the constant threat of the sea closing in are all everyday realities. Food, leave, and even onboard entertainment have long been ways for ships to function. Most U.S. ships in WWII had ice cream-making machines aboard. Even the submarines.

But the captain's role is to balance these tools of morale with his own unwavering authority. Some commanders are able to walk the line between high expectations and respect, admiration, and even love from a crew. However, none of these qualities are required by the Navy. A crew doesn't need to love or even like its captain. In fact, as far as the Navy is concerned, they can even despise him. But they do have to respect and obey him.

Janeway's investigation found Caldin to be an ineffective leader. But the investigation revealed more. Something was broken aboard the *Partridge*. Yes, the crew had lost confidence in the captain, but they had also lost their ability to function as a working ship. Removing Caldin and restoring ranks were just the beginning.

During Janeway's interviews with the officers and crew, a former officer continually came up. Men spoke of him so highly that Janeway made note of the name and filed a recommendation in his report.

As Jim White sat in the pub enjoying a celebratory round, he thought about how much he would miss the officers and crew from the *Owl*. Working on Bird Boats had its charms but it was time to move on. There would be an opportunity for another officer to lead the *Owl* and White was eager to cultivate a career in the Navy long after the war was over. Besides, maybe his new ship would have some of those modern amenities that caught his eye as a young recruit: an ice cream parlor or a barber shop.

But his dreams and his drink were interrupted by an urgent message from the ship. A sailor handed him an envelope saying that it had been delivered to the ship and all he was told was to put it in the Captain's hands as soon as possible.

The orders were to report to Captain Dayton Clark, the hardnosed commander of Force Mulberry. White wasted no time making his way to Clark's offices in Grosvenor Square. Clark, who looked like he hadn't slept in days, came right to the point:

"White, what are your plans?"

"I have orders to report to Miami," White answered. Observing Clark's glare, he wished he was there now.

"The hell you do. You're not going to Miami. You're staying here. I need to get rid of this crazy guy and you're going to take his place. You're the new captain of the *Partridge.*"

It would be the second time that White relieved Adnah Caldin from a Bird Boat.

"His manner was the opposite of Caldin's panicky behavior," Bill Ames recalled of White in a 2009 interview. "He was fair-minded and had a good understanding of what the crew had suffered under Caldin. The crew responded well and handled their duties with a refreshing efficiency. It was as if a weight had been lifted off of them and there was a crew that once again smiled as they carried out their assignments. White's calm, efficient, and encouraging manner rescued the crew. His style was the perfect antidote for Caldin."

It is a tantalizingly symmetrical story that pits time-tested tradition against young hotshots with new ideas from the civilian world. But many men were thrust into command during the war. Some were meant to lead and others were not. Most were not removed from duty.

It was neither a triumph of tradition or innovation that occurred aboard the *Partridge*. When Jim White stepped aboard to take command of the ship in 1944, there was only a sense of relief that the men could now perform their duty to their country unencumbered.

Jim White may have had bigger dreams than the *Partridge* but he didn't let them show. He would oversee a semblance of normalcy and calm amid the frenetic build-up to battle. He would ensure the meticulous execution of duties the ship was assigned. And he would balance fairness, discipline, and competence—all of which earned him respect and love from those who served under him decades later. But all of Jim White's natural skills as a leader could not save the *Partridge* from the random destruction that war, too often, brings.

Chapter 14
Our Whole World

The landings at Normandy on June 7, 1944, have entered the minds of many British, French, and Americans as a defining moment of the war. Although dozens of amphibious landings had been conducted in the Pacific and many great battles had been fought across Europe between Russian and German forces, Normandy was different. The landings represented both a political and propaganda necessity as well as a logistical miracle. Simply keeping Russia from negotiating a peace with Germany was a major reason for the landings to take place earlier than some planners thought prudent.

Normandy was a necessary step in the defeat of Germany and in defining the political map of Europe after the war that required far more than the courage of a handful of men storming the beaches. Unlike the landings of Iwo Jima, for example, where over 4,000 marines gave their lives defeating an enemy that had no hope of being resupplied, the men landing at Normandy would face a mobile, armored enemy that had a very real chance at knocking the entire invasion back into the ocean days, weeks, and even months after an initially successful landing.

In addition, the coordination between land, sea, and air forces was unprecedented in the history of warfare. While in both the Atlantic and Pacific Allied forces enjoyed superiority on the water and air, the tight confines of the English Channel made quick, sharp attacks from the Germans a real threat. In addition, fire from shore-based artillery, virtually a non-existent threat to the U.S. Navy in the Pacific, was a major problem to the auxiliary ships attempting to construct an artificial harbor that would make the entire invasion a success.

The result of all of these factors was an incredibly broad land, sea, and air battle that needed to be sustained for weeks and months. As troops moved further inland, suppressing German positions, tank and troop landing ships poured armor and men on to the beaches to increase pressure on the enemy. Ships began to cross the channel with the components of the Mulberry harbor. Small tugs, under fire, moved them into place. It wasn't until several weeks after June 7, 1944, that the harbor construction was complete.

For the *Partridge,* the initial D-Day landings saw the ship standing by to perform duties she had excelled at in the Caribbean: rescuing disabled ships at sea.

The opportunity came on June 6, 1944. The *Partridge* was ordered ahead of the invasion fleet. A British LCT (Landing Craft Tank) had struck an object underwater, rupturing its hull. The *Partridge* hooked up a tow and started for the beach. Slowly, however, the ship began to take on more water and sink. Getting to Normandy was impossible and instead White ordered the LCT removed from the area under protest from its angry captain.

On the way back, the *Partridge* crossed through the invasion armada departing from England.

"We threaded our way through this mass of ships," recalled Jim White. "And it was just an avalanche of vessels as far as the eye could see."

When they towed the LCT back to port, White asked why they had been sent out. It turned out that the *Partridge* was slated to be one of the first ships out in front of the armada. By rescuing the LCT, they had missed being in the vanguard of the invasion force.

"We really felt like we had dodged a bullet, not being one of the first ships in," recalled White.

This small footnote in the June 6 landings could have been the highlight of the ship's participation in the war—the big story shared at reunions for decades to come. As it turned out, the event passed into an obscure fact about the *Partridge* that not many remembered through the fog of what was to come.

Just before 2 AM on June 11, 1944, Mike Rich stared into the radar scope, viewing two blips that were moving slowly off the port quarter. He notified the bridge but then spotted a third object off the starboard side.

It was crowded in the Channel and Rich speculated that the ominous blips could be British ships not aware of the convoy delivering vital components to build a harbor off the Normandy. In fact, the danger of collision with friendly forces was, in many ways, more likely than an enemy attack. But Rich alerted the bridge of the possible threat and then took up a gun position on the upper deck. The ship's engines strained at nearly full power to tow the awkward three-span pontoon bridge toward France.

On that night the English Channel was a dangerous but strangely beautiful place. A land, sea, and air battled raged around the *Partridge,* but she had entered a calm eye of the storm. The horizon lit up in white flashes and low rumbles reverberated across the sea. An occasional eruption of machine gun fire or the buzz of aircraft engines brought the battle closer.

For now, all the men aboard the small ship plodding slowly through the water could do was soak it all in. It was a strange moment of peace for everyone aboard and for many it would be their last.

Danger for the *Partridge* did not lie in a spectacular sea battle. The real threat was either from a collision with a friendly vessel, as Mike Rich had feared, or from a lightning strike in the darkness similar to what had happened during the practice exercise *Tiger* at Slapton Sands.

This night the crew of the *Partridge* knew that German high-speed attack boats made regular runs in the Channel, usually from Le Havre to Brest, and that they were about to cross that route. They also knew that the *Partridge* was a slow-moving target while it was towing the massive floating pontoon bridge known as a *Whale.* Many hoped that the Germans would target the real prize she was towing: the structure that would support a stream of tanks to reinforce the beachhead and drive the invasion.

White had sounded General Quarters moments before because of some distant fire that didn't seem right. Because of White's actions, the ship stood at high alert as they came closer to the combat raging ashore in Normandy. Many stared transfixed by the distant battle on the horizon, with flashes and booms dampened by the distance between them. Bob Miller, a correspondent for the United Press, was aboard as a passenger. Miller had reported extensively on the invasion of Guadalcanal and had returned to the U.S. to recover from prolonged tropical illness. Now he was returning to cover the war in Europe and recorded his observations of an eerie calm as a battle raged in the dark night around the ship:

> *"I went on the bridge. Star shells were arching across the sky, rivaling the moon's brilliance. Miles astern the corvettes, destroyers, and MTBs were out searching for E-boats."*

> *"A destroyer flushed one of the quarries and there was an abrupt exchange of shots. Dull flashes split the darkness on the sea to our right. Red tracers streaked into the sky."*

> *"A plane flew high over our heads. There was a huge explosion somewhere astern with a great belching roar and a sudden huge gout of smoke."*

> *"I spoke to the men on the guns, glanced at the sky and uneasily down at the sea."*

Tom Buffum was below deck with a group of men ready to pass ammunition above deck, should it be needed. Usually, a crew feels safest above deck going into battle; however, on a small ship like the *Partridge,* no one could be sure where one would be safe. Even a small machine gun strafing could be highly destructive and the men with Buffum below deck felt a sense of security.

Bill Ames was on duty on the upper deck after checking in with some of the sailors he had placed in the pilot house. Among those half dozen sailors was George

Duncan, who had a widowed mother and a brother in the South Pacific. Johnny Scherer was there too. Scherer, who had helped create the *Partridge's* Donald Duck mascot, had just gotten married in his hometown of New York City before the *Partridge* left the States in December. Ames had secured positions in the pilot house for these men and a few other crew members he felt protective of.

"We all thought about Duncan's mother and Scherer's wife. There wasn't a safe place on the ship, but I felt like the pilot house was safer than above or below deck," recalled Ames, decades later.

In the meantime, Robert Miller, the UP reporter, continued to move around the deck, talking to the tense men standing at the ready on the *Partridge's* meager defenses. One of the men Miller may have spoken to was my grandfather. After returning home on leave a month later, he spoke to a local paper recounting that night:

> *Thurman Krouse was standing by his gun. His battle station had been changed the day before and he now knows that the lad who took his place was killed. Then the hit came...*

Al Riker from New Jersey remembered actually seeing the enemy ship, and gunners about to fire. Some men reported seeing a starburst shell revealing German E-boats, two off the port side and one off starboard. There is even a painting depicting the ship firing back at the E-boat as the torpedo makes its way toward the ship. Some of the surviving officers and crew don't recall any of these details—it all happened too fast for them. But the results were the same.

Two torpedoes struck the *Partridge*. The first hit the magazine and the second struck the engine room. It's likely that the first was the death blow to the ship. The torpedo strike and ignition of the ship's ordinance were nothing short of catastrophic. Miller recorded the initial impact:

> *"It tore into the ship's entrails. The whole ship shivered and then leapt. I went reeling down the deck, grabbing for a hold. Then a blinding flash like a photographic magnesium flare."*

The blind flash Miller saw was likely the ship's magazine exploding. In the darkness of night, the German E-boat managed to hit the small ship precisely where its destruction was assured.

Many men were killed instantly in the explosion. Ames' effort to protect the most vulnerable of the crew had failed. The pilot house was completely engulfed in the explosion and everyone in it killed instantly.

At the moment, however, Ames knew nothing of the fate of his crew mates. He, like many aboard the *Partridge*, was simply thrown clear of the ship by the explosion. He had a peculiar sensation of floating, serenely through the dark air above the Channel, sure that he had died in the blast. His peace was broken as he hit the sea and plunged deep into its cold blackness.

"I know that I was down deep enough that my impulse to give up and breath water kicked in just before I broke the surface," he recalled years later.

Mike Rich came to in the water just in time to see the ship roll over on its side and sink beneath the waves. He was left alone in the water with two broken legs and a severe head injury. Jim White was also thrown from the ship into the water. In fact, about half of the accounts of survivors tell some version of either being thrown into the air or waking up in the water.

The explosion was immense, but the *Partridge* stayed afloat for somewhere between 20 and 30 seconds. It wasn't a lot of time, but enough to save lives or scramble to try. Bob Miller, the UP reporter, witnessed the desperate final moments aboard as the ship began to sink:

> *"Sea water erupted all over the ship. I was temporarily blinded by filmy spray. I picked myself up with the others and found surprisingly, I was unhurt and that I had my glasses on and they were intact. [T]he deck's crazy slant showed that the ship was going down fast. Someone cried out: "The life raft—cut it loose." An unrecognizable figure crawled past on hands and knees, dragging a useless and dangling left leg behind him."*

That figure crawling past was likely Gunner's Mate Al Riker. Manning a gun on deck, Riker was thrown into the air when the ship was hit by the second torpedo. He crashed onto the main deck across the anchor engine, breaking his back in several places and legs in several places. The ship quickly sank beneath him amid a frenzy on the decks to get life rafts into the water. From Miller's report:

> *"Oily water moved up around our ankles. We began hacking agonizingly away at the bindings of the life raft as the ship began to settle. Abruptly it came loose and I plunged with the others onto a maze of ropes and debris tearing to free myself as the raft*

bobbed teasingly away—just out of reach. I had, I suppose, one more second. With a desperate lunge, I reached the raft and hauled myself on to it as the ship I had left rolled heavily over and then plunged, leaving boiling black bubbles on the sea as she went down."

The men above deck were the lucky ones. Although most sailors were topside or near topside when the torpedo hit, many crew members were trapped below deck, with no chance to make it to the surface. Gunner's Mate Al Schlais from Chicago reached into a hatch to extend a hand to a man pinned down below. With the ship sinking fast, listing badly and about to roll over, Schlais had to leave the sailor. Until he died in 2009, Schlais could recall with complete clarity the desperate look on the sailor's face.

Electrician's mate Dale Krinn from Ohio spotted a friend, fellow electrician W. A. Allen, trapped under a fallen spotlight. Trying to lift the light was futile. Like Schlais he was forced to leave the screaming, desperate man to drown.

My grandfather, a gunner's mate, managed to cut loose Richard "Chino" Melanson. The hometown paper in Chewsville, Maryland, reported his calm exit from the ship:

"He resisted the temptation to jump overboard (some of the men who did so were killed); instead, he stayed with the ship almost to the last and then calmly slid into the water."

"He was still 'clicking' and knew that the important thing to save his neck was for him to swim quickly

away from the ship so he would not be dragged down by the current resulting from the boat going under. As he swam he looked back once and saw the last of the Partridge. He says now it was as though his home were disappearing..."

Plunging into the sea is a sudden and terrifyingly vulnerable feeling. Almost completely helpless, groups of sailors clung together, fighting against injuries sustained during the ship's destruction, hypothermia, and the enemy. Miller's UP story recalls the terror and helplessness of sailors suddenly without a ship in the dark night:

"Thick, choking oil covered the water like syrup, clogging my ears and nose and matting my hair. The night was alive with sound. Men were shouting. Others called for help. There were odd cries of encouragement and the occasional moans of the injured. Men were crammed on the raft and all around it, some clinging to the sides. We saw a sudden great black shape knifing through the sea. Together we bawled and screamed. But the ship passed in the night."

In the Chewsville account, there is mention of a German attack on survivors in the water, although this has not been verified in any of the official reports or first-hand accounts:

"Although they tried to stay together and encourage each other as they floated and swam, when the Germans opened fire on the survivors, those who were able, swam as fast as they could to the bridge

the Partridge had been towing. Thurman says he had been in the water about 45 minutes when he finally made it to the bridge and despite the oil covered surface of everything—himself, the water, the bridge—he half climbed and was half pulled to safety."

Like my grandfather, many found salvation on the Whale unit, pulling themselves up or being pulled up. Bill Ames, with a severe back injury as a result of either the initial explosion or impact to the water, was grabbed and hoisted aboard. He collapsed on the deck and passed out from exhaustion and shock.

Mike Rich made it to a raft of debris so full of survivors that it was almost completely submerged in the water. Rich spotted Joe Cooney unconscious, cradled in the arms of several other sailors on a makeshift raft. Joe Shannon came to underwater assuming that the gray void was the afterlife. After breaking the surface and hearing voices he realized that he was still alive. Hearing men screaming in pain, he called out:

"Stop screaming and start praying."

It was only at this point that Shannon noticed that his arm was broken and almost unusable. After finding a piece of mast he pulled his lame arm around it and stuck it into his pocket. He grabbed the body of a sailor who floated past. Shannon wasn't sure if he was dead or alive. It turned out to be Lloyd Beale, one of only five African American sailors aboard the ship, and he was still breathing. With his free hand, Shannon pulled Beale in and kept him afloat. Then he heard a strange sound. The men he had heard screaming had stopped. Now they were singing.

Tom Buffum spent his first moments in the water rescuing others. He found the relative safety of some floating debris and then swam out to men crying for help in the frigid water, pulling them back safety. Wounded himself, Buffum's strong swimming skills helped men who could barely keep afloat in the oily, cold water. After they were assembled at the raft, he realized that the men around him were succumbing to shock. Some were becoming physically ill and many were shaking violently.

Most were sure that they were going to die in the cold water of the channel. As the senior officer in the group, he was faced with panicked questions about their survival that he simply couldn't answer. He decided the best thing they could do was to sing and encourage others to do the same.

Buffum's clear baritone voice singing Quaker hymns cut through the darkness to the men around him and to others floating in the frigid water. Hymns like *How Can I Keep From Singing?* rang out in the dark night:

> *My life flows on in endless song;*
> *Above earth's lamentation,*
> *I hear the sweet, tho' far-off hymn*
> *That hails a new creation;*
> *Thro' all the tumult and the strife*
> *I hear the music ringing;*
> *It finds an echo in my soul—*
> *How can I keep from singing?*

"When I first heard him, I couldn't believe it," recalled Shannon. "Here we were in the water and I thought: 'My God, they're singing! Are they crazy?' But he really raised everyone's spirits. He really came into his own that night."

Shannon joined the singing. It was an effort that pushed the group back from the brink of despair and pain just long enough to hold on. Unlike men lost at sea in the Pacific or North Atlantic, the prospect of being lost for a long time was unlikely in the Channel. The waters were so crowded with ship traffic; in fact, the survivors from the *Partridge* feared mostly the great dark ship's profiles that sped through the night toward the battle taking place just over the horizon. They were more likely to be run down by a friendly ship than fall prey to the enemy.

Al Riker floated helplessly in the water, unable to move from the injuries to his back and legs in the explosion. John Fay, a sailor from New York City, dragged him aboard the Whale unit, not knowing how severely injured he was. Both were shocked to find his leg at an unnatural right angle, but he was, at least, out of the water and relatively safe.

Fay and Riker were now on a floating platform and were joined by other sailors who were finding their way to their safe haven. For men on the Whale Unit, seeking rescue was the next immediate concern. My grandfather and his shipmates stood on the exposed, motionless structure, wet, cold, and without a clue about what would happen next. Men were crying out in pain or simply unconscious all around them. Some dead and some dying. Hours went by with only silhouettes of ships passing them in the distance. Help, if it ever came, might be too late considering the condition of men like Riker.

Joe Shannon (known as Joe Nutt at the time) prior to shipping out with the Partridge in 1943

After several hours, the men spotted the lights from an approaching ship, but they were far from elated. No one knew if it was a friendly ship or the enemy. My grandfather produced a sidearm and began to check to see if it was loaded. Don Wampler, thinking more clearly, looked at the gun in astonishment:

"What are you going to do with that?"

"If it's the Germans..." said my grandfather, still checking the firearm.

"You're going to throw that thing overboard now. If it's the Germans, we're going to surrender."

My grandfather, coming to his senses, tossed the pistol overboard. Then they waited to see who was closing in on them.

Petty Officer Robert Ainslie aboard the Canadian ship HMCS *Prescott* witnessed a huge explosion on the horizon during the morning of June 11.

"We had left the French coast early that morning and were on submarine duty," recalled Ainsle. "After the explosion, it came down from the captain that he thought a ship had been hit and we were to go investigate. We lowered our scramble nets and started off toward the explosion. As I recall it took us quite a while to get there."

The *Prescott* was a corvette, a ship not much larger than the *Partridge.* Canadian corvettes were hastily put into commission as smaller warships that could screen convoys and help fight the U-boat threat. On that morning, the fastest she could travel toward the wreck of the *Partridge* was 16 knots.

Ainslie recalled the grisly scene when they arrived near to the wreck at dawn:

"The engines were cut and we were sort of just drifting in quietly. We started pulling bodies aboard. Some were alive and some were dead. All of them were covered in oil. We had sick bay attendants on board that were trying to take care of those guys as much as we could. We were told we only had about 2 or 3 minutes. There was still the threat from the E-boats and submarines. Staying still like we were wasn't a good idea."

Joe Shannon felt this urgency when he was rescued by the Canadians. Still holding Lloyd Beale, the Canadian sailors urged Shannon to let him go.

"They kept telling me that he was dead, and I yelled back 'He's not dead!'"

Shannon refused to leave the water until they took Beale aboard. When they did, Shannon's injuries immediately became apparent.

"I took two steps on deck and fell flat on my face," recalled Shannon. Among his other injuries, he had two shattered knees.

Dalton Kirkman, the sailor from North Carolina who had spent a leave home with my grandfather, had a typical experience of blacking out in the water and gaining consciousness aboard the *Prescott.*

The crew from the *Prescott* rescued who they could find and headed back to Omaha beach at Normandy. There, they dropped off the survivors. The severely wounded would be treated on the beach at a makeshift hospital inside a large tank landing craft (LST).

Shannon remembered the Normandy beaches as a reminder of the wider war that the *Partridge* was taking part in.

"It was filled with bodies. Some were covered in tarps and some weren't. There were wounded, dead, and dying all around. They shot me full of morphine and then I blacked out."

After dropping off survivors, the *Prescott* took the bodies with her and left for the open channel. Ainslie, along with other members of the crew, had the grisly task of wrapping the bodies in canvass and weighting them for burial at sea. The ship drifted in the channel with cut engines. The Captain came out on the deck to perform a brief ceremony. The bodies were then buried at sea, including Lloyd Beale, who Shannon had held all morning, and Charlie Doyle, who had been saved from the paint locker by his fellow crew members just a month earlier.

Jim White lay on the deck of the *Prescott,* unconscious from a severe blow to the head that had cracked his skull. When he opened his eyes, he saw the face of Joe Cooney lying beside. Canadian sailors were drawing a tarp over his face.

"We all thought you'd be the one that wouldn't make it through the night," said one of the Canadian sailors.

Members of the Partridge crew had pushed Cooney's unconscious body onto a raft of floating debris, hoping to save him. Now the man that had helped them through so many trying times was gone, along with the ship many of them called home. All told, a third of the crew were dead. The rest were scattered throughout the war zone of the Battle of Normandy.

Chapter 15
Measure of War

Joe Shannon woke up to see an angel sitting on the foot of his bed. He watched her lovely, fine features in a milky white light for what seemed like hours, not having the courage or the inclination to move. As in a dream, he couldn't seem to muster the strength to move or speak. Was he held silent by some unseen force or did his body simply want to enjoy the quiet peace of the room?

The last memories he had were disconnected: in the water, in terrible pain, on a beach with hundreds of dead and wounded, then the quick sweet black blanket that morphine brought.

The pieces began to fall together and he gathered strength to speak:

"Am I dead?"

The angel turned to look at him. A human look of surprise and anxiety came over her face. She didn't speak. She only hurried out of the room.

When a group of doctors and nurses returned, he learned the truth. He was not dead and he was not in heaven. Shannon had been in a coma for over a month. He was in a hospital being closely watched as one of the many casualties returning from across the Channel. When he entered the general ward he was greeted by cheers from a group of wounded Army Rangers who had been tracking his progress. Listening to Axis Sally report on the invasion fleet, they heard that the *Partridge* had gone down with all hands.

"Lay down, Joe, you're supposed to be dead!" a Ranger called out.

Shannon's wounds were extensive: shrapnel embedded throughout his body including in his head, a severe concussion, a broken nose, a broken arm, a broken collar bone, two shattered knees, and burns across the left half of his body, including his face and lips. He would be treated at several hospitals in London, survive a V1 rocket attack, and eventually fully recover at a Naval hospital in Philadelphia.

"That V1 destroyed a wing of the hospital that Jim White and Mike Rich were in the day before. So they sort of dodged it a second time."

Mike Rich had made it back to England with two broken legs and a fractured skull. Being thrown clear from the sinking ship, Rich found himself in the darkness of the water, alone. He pulled his body through the oily water using only his arms, eventually finding a group of men on a raft. Not able to pull himself aboard, Rich held on for several hours until the *Prescott* arrived.

Tom Buffum, recovering in a British hospital, wrote home to his parents, casually mentioning the possibility of some kind of medal that might be awarded. It turned out to be the Navy and Marine Corp Medal, the highest non-combat award for bravery in the United States military. His citation reads:

> For heroic conduct as a Member of the Crew of the USS. Partridge when she was torpedoed and sunk on June 11,1944, off the French Coast. Although

wounded, lieutenant (then lieutenant, junior grade) Buffum grouped a number of his men together in the water and, personally saving the lives of two men who were drowning, kept his group calm until the arrival of rescue craft two hours later. His leadership, courage and endurance upheld the highest traditions of the United States Naval Service.

Bill Ames sustained substantial injuries to his legs when the ship sank, requiring extensive surgeries across the United States over the course of two years. His surgeries and long hospital stays in New York and Boston allowed him to keep in touch with many of the crew mates who were largely from the Northeast. At times he visited families that had lost husbands, sons, and brothers when the ship went down, including the family of Johnny Scherer and his widowed bride in New York City. She had been married to Scherer for seven months.

Dalton Kirkman was listed as Missing In Action. A widower, Kirkman had left two daughters with his parents to join the Navy. When the girls got the news they locked themselves in the bathroom, hysterical that both parents had been taken from them. But Kirkman had survived. With two arms in casts, he had to dictate a note to his family to deliver them the news that he was alive.

Jim White, too, was severely injured, drifting in and out of consciousness in the weeks after the sinking. The final report of the ship's demise is written by Tom Buffum because White's injuries were too extensive to allow him to file the report. In all, it lists five men as dead and over 30 missing. All of the dead were buried at sea and the missing bodies were never recovered.

Jim White recovering from wounds in England

For most of the survivors, the *Partridge* was the last ship they would serve on. Injuries from the violent explosion were severe requiring multiple surgeries, long recoveries, and ultimately led to discharge papers.

Like many veterans of WWII who survived close brushes with death, they built something that made their luck worth it. Some in the military. Some as corporate leaders. Many as working men raising families. As the years passed on, their experience on the *Partridge* became just one moment in their lives. But one that they were linked to no matter where else they served, what jobs they held, how they succeeded or failed.

Joe Feeney returned with a broken leg and was soon discharged from the Navy. He returned to South Boston and immediately took up his old hobby of sailing his small boat dubbed *Sailbad the Sinner*. He was joined one afternoon in the summer of 1945 by Bill Ames who was in Boston undergoing further treatment from his injuries. The two war buddies enjoyed sailing tranquil waters again.

In 1948, Feeney, now a fireman in Boston, finally got around to marrying Betty, the girl he had written to so often during the war. The wedding was attended by Joe Meskll, Bill Marrick, Stan Menard, Tom Buffum, Bill Ames, Tim Donovan, and Paul Walton. They all enjoyed this unofficial reunion and agreed on a more official one to be held the following year in New York City.

It was a simple affair. A hall was rented. Beer was served. There were decorations and a recreation of the *Partridge* mascot emblem. Photos show a group of old friends relaxing and sharing stories. But these men are grown up, some with wives and children and other lives. It was a period of hope and renewal that was reflected in the rest of the country. The war was over and young lives were picking up where they had left off.

Looking at the photographs, there are a few reminders of the loss these men suffered. One is the absence of my grandmother. The years after the war were difficult for my grandfather, who suffered from some degree of post-traumatic stress. Like many men who returned with nightmares and short-tempers and a nervous sense of unease, my grandfather would never be normal again. My grandmother preferred to think the war was over. Attending reunions wasn't part of the post-war she had planned.

And she certainly wasn't alone in the thought. The reunion of 1949, like most, was the last for many years. Until age and reflection prodded some of the men to dig and find something in their past experience that was worth preserving and remembering. After the marriages, divorces, children, grandchildren, careers, accolades, illnesses, retirements, financial struggles and successes, this wasn't just another piece of their lives; it was their great adventure. Their defining moment.

None of that reflection is in the 1949 reunion photos. They are gathered like high school friends home from college. Life is ahead, bright and sunny. Everyone is good-looking and skinny, in style and full of youthful bravado. They had won the war and a rental hall, a keg of beer, and a little music were their modest spoils.

But the second absence from the party would have been more conspicuous than that of my grandmother: Jim White didn't return in New York City in 1949 to see his shipmates. In fact, he wouldn't see his shipmates until 40 years later. White stated that he never felt guilty about the ship sinking because he firmly believed that sounding general quarters just prior to the attack saved many lives. Still, his injuries and abrupt end to his naval career made life difficult. White hit a self-described 'rough patch' and it would be many decades before he could face his past again.

From the *Titanic* to the *Arizona*, narratives of sinking ships have entered literature and history as almost a genre of their own. The sheer size of many ships turns their demise into a slow-motion human drama played out in hours and, sometimes, in days as the conventional world recreated aboard a ship slowly turns in on itself and succumbs to the pressures of the sea that have been lurking outside all along. In the *Partridge's* own history, the sinking of the *Lihue* saw what was essentially a floating warehouse of airplane engines and GM trucks lurch and list and then suddenly turn on end and plunged into the sea.

Part of what fuels these narratives are the interiors of ships that serve as deceptively stable environments for those who make them home. But the security and stability of that home are a delusion. The *Partridge,* which had sailed the oceans of the world for nearly 25 years and was home to over 90 men, sank in less than 30 seconds. Many men aboard thought of it as less than a sinking and more of a sudden and abrupt destruction of the world beneath their feet.

Years later, in advanced age, Jim White would recall the dynamic at a reunion he did finally attend. Sitting on a vessel similar in size to the *Partridge*, White recalled:

"This was our whole world. And in an instant, it was gone."

After 1949 there wasn't another reunion until the late 1980s. The small group received a newsletter put together by Bill Ames and his wife Dotty. Ames urged his fellow crew mates to stay in touch not only for sentimental reasons but in case any of them needed verification of their injuries due to the sinking for administrative purposes. Ames even supplied the duck mascot with each newsletter, which he created using clip art images from his local library in Milwaukee.

But in an age before email, Facebook, and Twitter, it proved too expensive and too much effort to keep it going and the monthly issues went on hiatus in the early Fifties.

Some small subgroups stayed in touch. But the *Partridge* passed into history as a small ship performing a small part in the war in the Caribbean and during the Battle for Normandy.

Don Jaeger, killed in action off Normandy,
one of the creators of the Donald Duck mascot for the Partridge.

Eddie and Gina Ward. Eddie Ward was killed in action off Normandy.

After a period of recovery in Britain, Joe Shannon was shipped back to the U.S. for further treatment in a Philadelphia Navy hospital. While there he became friends with a group of Marines wounded in the Battle of Saipan who invited him to a reunion after the war.

Later, in 1954, Joe was surprised to see one of the marines he became good friends on the film screen. His name was Lee Marvin and the film was *The Caine Mutiny*. But more than seeing his friend on the screen, Joe was taken with how the *Caine's* story so closely tracked that of the *Partridge*. And Joe wasn't the only one.

Don Wampler contacted my grandfather after seeing *The Caine Mutiny*. The behavior exhibited by Queeg, the fact that the *Caine* was a minesweeper, and Queeg's relief from command were all familiar to Wampler and to other men from the crew. But the most anyone could do was shrug their shoulders and move on. For most, school, careers, family, and homes were their future. The war was something to be left behind.

And yet stories of *Caine* as well as the ship's demise kept ties between the men over the years. Finally in the late 1980s Joe Shannon, inspired by the reunion of the Marines he was hospitalized with just after the war, would bring together a much smaller and much older group of men who had served aboard the *Partridge* for a few last reunions. The first of these was in New Orleans, and this time Jim White was there, finally able to put to bed the demons that had plagued him for years. The remaining men welcomed him back warmly just as they had in in 1944, talking about the *Partridge,* Normandy, and *The Caine Mutiny*.

Joe Shannon receiving the Purple Heart in November of 1944

*Jim White receiving the Purple Heart for injuries sustained
when the Partridge was sunk off Normandy*

Chapter 16
Strawberries and Ball Bearings

The points where the *Caine* and the *Partridge* overlap are striking: a dilapidated minesweeper in the U.S. Navy during World War II had a captain relieved of command in the middle of combat operations and found to be incompetent and is replaced by a lieutenant named Jim White.

But Herman Wouk has gone out of his way to emphasize that he didn't base Queeg on any captain he served under or any one story. In his forward to *Caine*, Wouk underscores these points emphatically:

> *This is a work of fiction in the historical setting of World War II. It contains errors of fact. Times and places of specific circumstance in actual military operations, names and missions of ships, and naval communication procedures have been distorted either to suit the story or to avoid inadvertent recounting of still-classified information. All the persons and events aboard the Caine are imaginary. Any resemblance to actual persons or events are coincidental. No ship named the USS Caine exists or existed. The records of thirty years show no instance of court-martial resulting from the relief of a captain at sea under*

Articles 184, 185, and 186 of the Navy Regulations. The fictitious figure of the deposed captain was contrived from a study of psychoneurotic case histories to motivate the central situation and is not a part of a real military person or a type. This statement is made in view of an existing tendency to seek lampoons of living people in fiction. The author served under two captains of the regular Navy in three years aboard destroy-minesweepers, both of whom were decorated for valor.

In other words, Queeg is based on a broad collection of incidents and traits. He is not a person so much as a profile. And that person never existed. If Wouk did hear about the *Partridge*, it only informed a small piece of the overall *Caine* story.

Be that as it may, the absence of mutiny and a trial did not stop the mainstream press from comparing the USS *Vance* to *Caine* during the Vietnam War. The *Vance* was a small destroyer escort participating in *Operation Market Time,* which involved searching for smuggled contraband that might help the Vietcong. The captain of the *Vance,* Marcus Aurelius Arnheiter, was a quirky demagogue whose escapades caused officers to begin a "Mad Marcus" log that was effectually used to relieve Arnheiter from command.

Time magazine's *The Arnheiter Incident* places the incident among some hefty literary company: "From Herman Melville's Captain Vere (who hanged Billy Budd) to Herman Wouk's Captain Queeg (who rolled ball bearings during *The Caine Mutiny*), naval literature overflows with tales of rumbustious skippers and mutinous crewmen."

Later, in the same article, an officer from the *Vance* is quoted as saying: "We all have a little of Captain Queeg in us...but Arnheiter had more than his share."

Arnheiter eventually had his day in court, bringing a lawsuit for libel and slander against Neil Sheehan for his book *The Arnheiter Affair*. The book was removed from print after Arnheiter won the suit. Arnheiter was adamant about a conspiracy of officers to undermine his authority.

If Caldin had "a day in court" he most certainly would have leveled the same charges against the crew and officers who wrote mocking poems about him and discussed taking matters to a higher authority. Counter to this would have been charges of poor ship handling, poor management skills, and even cowardice for fleeing the bridge when the ship was in crisis.

All of this aside, however, there are two talismans that could have proven the *Partridge* as the inspiration for *The Caine Mutiny*: strawberries and ball bearings. Queeg famously turns the ship upside down in order to find strawberries and also possesses a nervous twitch of rolling two ball bearings over and over in his hand.

But strawberries and ball bearings remain elusive in researching this book. Accounts from the *Partridge* crew recall many details about Caldin but none mention strawberries or ball bearings directly. Third-hand stories (from children and grandchildren) do mention the famous strawberry incident (some others recall canned peaches) and ball bearings or some similar twitch. None of these, however, can be verified.

But what else is known of Queeg? Aside from his signpost actions, the yellow stain, the cut tow line, the strawberries, the ball bearings—we don't know anything about him. In fact, we know the careers and motivations of just about everyone else aboard the *Caine*. Willie is the rich kid coming of age. Keefer is the intellectual trapped in a bureaucratic hell. Maryk is the able fisherman with ambitions to make it in the Navy. But Queeg? We know he's a career Navy man who has come from the Atlantic escorting convoys. Other than his actions aboard the *Caine* we know little else. Comparably, we know a wealth of information about Adnah Caldin. His upbringing, expectations, high hopes, failure, and homecoming. Insert his backstory to Queeg and a fully drawn central anti-hero emerges. Instead of looking for evidence of Queeg in Caldin, it's ultimately more fruitful to look for Caldin in Queeg.

I began research for this book by interviewing surviving crew members. Talking nearly 65 years after events, not one crew member could recall Caldin's name off the top of their head. Most who remembered his name had to guess at the spelling. All, however, recalled his actions. Some with laughter, some with passion and, in some cases, with bitter anger that cracked their voices with emotion. All could recall individual confrontation with him and details of shipboard life. But, like most personal conflict, none knew a shred of detail about his life before the *Partridge*. Most knew that he was transferred to land duty afterward, but the path went cold after that.

Strawberries and ball bearings would codify Caldin's life and solidify him as "the real Queeg." But real life is far more complicated than that. Even the Navy bureaucracy, so often parodied and vilified in film and literature. doesn't exist in black and white in reality. Court martial scenes abound with valiant heroes testifying, clever lawyers breaking down witnesses, and right triumphing against the hard wall of naval code. But this too has a softer edge. Edward Janeway, for example, was a civilian amateur yachtsman and stockbroker who was given authority to investigate the conduct of a career Navy officer. In fact, the entire operation of Mulberry put an extraordinary value in the expertise and, apparently, opinions of reserve officers, none of whom, it seems, ran into anything like a wall of stoic Navy tradition.

And Caldin doesn't exist solely in the *Partridge's* narrative as a sounding board for other personalities, motivations, and egos aboard the ship. He was a man who wanted, desperately, to succeed. Great expectations from wealthy family friends, a chance at youthful glory in the First World War, an attempt at higher education in the Eastern establishment, submarine school and a rapid advancement and wartime officers commission— these were all signs of, if not a stellar career, at least a respectable one.

But all of this came crashing down in one crucial test that only the Navy can bring on a man: command at sea. The captain of a ship, unlike the leader of a platoon or regiment, has absolute authority and absolute responsibility. Caldin may have been so eager to succeed that he took his responsibility too seriously. In trying to discipline the crew he simply lost respect and control. He also lost confidence—that critical turn that often ends careers. And Caldin may have been trying to do more than advance a Navy career. His aversion to the debauched life he knew from growing up in a hotel/saloon may have translated into an overeager ambition to clean up similar behaviors aboard the *Partridge*.

And what about the crew? Joe Cooney exists as the best parallel to the character of Joe Maryk—both were from New York, both had working experience of small craft at sea in ferry and tug boats in one case and fishing vessels in the case of the second. However, Joe Cooney had no desire to continue a career in the Navy; he was there to serve his country during the war and then go home. The dynamic between Queeg/Maryk and Caldin/Cooney still stands: it was the conflict between competent seamanship and unchecked ambition that fostered animosity toward the captain up and down the ranks. Wampler's poem is the closest to the Yellow Stain song—not mocking Caldin's courage so much as his harsh treatment of the crew and officers.

But the exercise in finding a point for point match between the two ships and their crews is ultimately fruitless. For every match, there are gaps in the stories as well. The ships were in different oceans, different theaters of war, and on different missions. But there is one more thread that ties the two ships together and brings Herman Wouk to a much closer proximity to the *Partridge.*

Chapter 17
Two Ships

In December of 1944, the *ATR-79* was commissioned into the U.S. Navy. It was a newly constructed Attack Rescue Tug built for a crew of 55 and five officers. She was immediately sent to the Pacific. After a brief stop in Florida, the ship sailed through the Panama Canal, reported to San Diego, and then sailed for Pearl Harbor. Her Executive Officer was a young lieutenant who recently reported for duty after serving in the Atlantic. His name was Tom Buffum.

Buffum would have been an exciting figure aboard the newly commissioned workship. The charismatic young officer had been involved in the D-Day invasion, saw action that resulted in the loss of his ship, and had plenty of stories to tell about acts of heroism, injury, and a harrowing rescue. He had been awarded the highest non-combat decoration for his actions during that incident. In short, Buffum had tales to tell and plenty of young officers and enlisted men around him who had yet to see combat and were eager to hear them.

Just before the ship arrived in Pearl Harbor on April 11, the *ATR-79* was crippled by an unexpected engine problem. The ship required a new IP piston that needed to be delivered from the manufacturer. She would be moored at Pearl for over three weeks. These events would be unremarkable in the story of the *Partridge* save for one fact: during the same three weeks the DMS *Southard* also arrived and, on April 25, a young Lieutenant Herman Wouk became her Executive Officer. The *Southard* and the *ATR-79* remained in Pearl Harbor docked in close proximity for several weeks.

It's easy to imagine a conversation between the two XOs. Both served on similarly sized ships, performing similar duties, and both had recently seen action. Wouk had just left the USS *Zane,* which participated in the Marshall and Sullivan Island campaigns. During the campaign in New Georgia (known as Operation Toenails), the *Zane* ran aground within range of Japanese artillery and was saved by the USS *Rail*, one of the Bird Boats of the same class as the *Partridge.*

Granted, Pearl Harbor was and still is a major U.S. Naval base, and it would have been a tangle of activity. But the two would have another chance to meet. After Pearl Harbor, both ships went their separate ways. *ATR-79* performed missions in and around the Philippines while the *Southard* participated in activities around the invasion and capture of Okinawa.

It was in October of that year, just over a month after the Japanese surrendered, that U.S. Forces in the Pacific were hit by an unusually turbulent series of tropical storms and typhoons. In September 1945, Typhoon *Ida* struck—severely damaging Buffum's ship to the point that it was dead in the water. The *ATR-79* had to be towed to Buckner Bay, Okinawa, where, by coincidence, the USS *Southard* was operating.

No sooner was the *ATR-79* repaired, but another, far more powerful typhoon hit: *Louise.* Both *ATR-79* and the *Southard* were in Buckner Bay during the storm. In the end, Buffum's ship would ride out the storm while Wouk's ship was grounded.

During this time, Buffum and Wouk spent a total of 20 days together in the vicinity of Buckner Bay, Okinawa.

Placing Wouk and the story of the *Partridge* in proximity throughout the entire U.S. Navy during WWII is a practice in impossible odds. But the field narrows quite a bit in Pearl Harbor and even further in Buckner Bay. Placing the story between two officers, both Ivy League graduates who were the same age, rank, and served in the same capacity aboard similar ships performing similar duties turns those odds on their head.

Wouk and Buffum, could have struck up a conversation on any number of topics. Their ships. Shared experiences in the war. Maybe college life at Columbia and Brown. If they met on Okinawa, the typhoon. They certainly would have talked about commanding officers at some point. And if they spoke about commanding officers, Caldin would have absolutely been a topic of conversation.

In Herman Wouk's memo to the Secretary of the Navy, he speaks about officers swapping stories in clubs throughout the Atlantic and Pacific. It's easy to imagine Wouk and Buffum in one of these officers' clubs or at a supply depot, having conversations about their war. Knowing about Buffum's decoration, Wouk may have asked about the sinking of the *Partridge*. Knowing that Wouk was already a published author, Buffum may have smiled thinking of Caldin and said what is often said to writers: "Have I got a great story to tell to you. It'd probably make a great novel."

If officers' clubs throughout the Pacific were rife with the Captain Bligh stories that Wouk outlined in his memo to the Secretary of the Navy, Tom Buffum's story had to be one of the best.

Chapter 18
The Captain's Wife

December 7, 1946

Dear Mr. Secretary:

On June 12, 1944, my husband, then Lieutenant Adnah N. Caldin, received a communication from you wherein he was reduced in rank from lieutenant, senior grade, to the permanent rank of Chief Boatswain.

The sound of a typewriter rang out from a home study in Virginia. At the keys was the wife of a Navy officer who had spent many years in many houses left alone to raise a child. At times, when her husband had steady shore or harbor duty, the family led a more or less normal life. But then duty at sea called and she would once again be met with loneliness and uncertainty, matched by an independence not otherwise permitted in the household.

When WWII began, experienced men to lead ships were in short supply. While the dangers were real, the opportunities for Navy officers to serve at a higher rank were greatly expanded. Caldin, who had seemed stuck permanently in his current rank, suddenly was promoted to lieutenant with his own command.

But now the war was over, and writing a letter was about the most Louise Caldin could do for her husband who she felt was wronged by the Navy he had served nearly his entire life. She made her concise, well-worded appeal directly to the Secretary of the Navy—arguing that, on the eve of D-Day, her husband had been treated unfairly and his humiliation and anger had found their way home.

"The incident which resulted in his reduction in rank arose out of his loyalty to his country in time of war and the execution of his duty as he perceived it in light of his many years of service in the Navy."

"When the circumstances of this case are reviewed, it becomes obvious that the incident arose as the result of long and trying service under war-time conditions resulting in what is commonly referred to as 'war nerves.'"

"The reduction in rank vitally affected my husband and his family inasmuch as the Navy was his career as distinguished from that duty imposed upon the citizens of this country during the duration of the war only."

"I feel that nearly a quarter of a century of faithful and honorable service to one's country merits the Department's consideration, and again I respectfully request that his case may be reviewed in light of all of the attending circumstances."

When held up against the many sacrifices made during the war, this one wrong may seem insignificant. But the Captain's wife attempted to be heard above the pain of loss and the joy of lives returned to normal at the war's end.

This request is made without knowledge on the part of my husband and without his consent. I have every reason to believe that he would disapprove of my making this request and for this reason I have refrained from doing so for the past two years. However, in view of the effect of the incident on him and his family, I feel that out of a sense of fair play that it should be called to the attention of the Department.

Respectfully submitted,
Mrs. A. N. Caldin

For Louise Caldin, the war wasn't quite over yet. As she mailed the letter, she hoped to restore to her husband some of the optimism and pride he had drawn from his years of service and promotion to ship's captain. Writing the letter threatened her husband's career as well as the peace of her marriage. She wasn't only reaching into a past her husband preferred to forget— she was probing into something the naval bureaucracy also preferred to leave behind in the chaos of war.

Mrs. Caldin's letter to the Navy represents the endgame in Adnah Caldin's struggle aboard the USS *Partridge*.

Every captain inherits his crew. They are his to shape and form, but they are also a unique collection of individuals. The crew Caldin inherited was coming off of a long, hard-fought campaign in the Caribbean, where they served under two capable captains. Would they need stronger discipline as they crossed over the Atlantic to participate in the invasion of Europe? Would the officers need to be prepared for dangers other than U-boat attacks? Was the crowded crew of the Lapwing minesweeper too familiar with their officers? Was nearly 25 years of naval experience worth more than the opinions of some reservist officers?

Lucy Caldin Wagenar, Caldin's only child, had few memories of her father's wartime years. She mostly remembered the day that he returned home. How he returned or why didn't much matter to a seven-year-old. It's easy to forget, in the midst of war stories full of risk, courage, and sacrifice, that there also are husbands, wives, sons, daughters, mothers, and fathers.

Had Adnah Caldin remained in command of the *Partridge* there is no telling if he would have survived its sinking or if the ship would have been sunk at all. The nature of war is pure chaos and it is only the neat lines of Hollywood that lead us to believe that happy endings only come to our heroes. The truth is that the Captain Blighs and Queegs had families that loved them and would see any debate about their naval career as secondary to the joy they felt having them home and safe at last.

Millions of stories came out of World War II. For Lucy Caldin, the greatest war story was the one about the day her dad came home from it and life returned to as normal as she knew it.

After the *Partridge* was sunk, Captain White had a chance encounter with Caldin in Norfolk. He reported at a reunion in the 1990s that Caldin had heard about the ship's demise and asked with great concern about the men who were killed or injured. Joe Shannon recalled a similar encounter with his former captain.

"Caldin said 'If I had been in charge, we would have gone down fighting.' What did he think we did?"

But the contradiction should come as no surprise. There are few villains in this story. Caldin's leadership may have been questionable, but his desire to do well and serve his country are above reproach.

However, in the eyes of the Navy, the stain of Caldin being relieved of command meant that any promotion in the future was unlikely. After so many years of hard work in the peacetime Navy, Caldin saw his golden opportunity to shine in a wartime command dissipate in his hands. He had begun to drink heavily and neared retirement with tired distraction that took its toll on his performance duties and his family life.

Louise Caldin must have been thrilled when she received a letter addressed to her from the U.S. Navy. The letter was dated December 16, 1946—a response amazingly quick considering the volume of correspondence that must have been moving through the office regarding the millions of men and women still overseas.

But the letter was short and cut her impassioned pleas for reconsideration with cold hard facts of bureaucracy. Yes, there had been an investigation, held on the brink of the D-Day invasion. And, yes, Adnah Caldin had been hastily reduced in rank. But then the letter pulled back giving a full bird's eye view of the Navy's post-war situation:

> *Subsequent to the cessation of hostilities of September 1945, a great many chief warrants, warrant officers, and enlisted personnel who held*

appointments for temporary service in higher commissioned grades, have been reverted to their permanent ranks and ratings. This has not been in the nature of disciplinary action, but solely because of a lack of billets in the shrinking naval establishments. Hence, it is unlikely that anything which might be revealed by further investigation at this time would in any way alter or change the present status of Chief Boatswain Caldin. All facts and circumstances pertaining to this case were carefully considered at the time of Mr. Caldin's hearing, and the case is now deemed to be closed.

It's understandable why many temporary ranks were reverted back to permanent status after the war. There just were not enough ships or command posts. But the letter implies that Caldin's hearing and reduction in rank were related somehow to this post-war activity. Its reference in the letter was more than likely meant to be comforting as well as intimidating. Millions of men were coming home. Life was returning to normal. Case closed.

But the final paragraph acknowledges the permanent damage that Caldin's hearing had done to his career:

If future legislation and the needs of the naval service permit appointment of commissioned warrant and warrant officers to higher commissioned grades in the postwar Navy, Chief Boatswain Caldin may then apply for such appointment, in which a full review will be made of his entire record, including the circumstances leading up to the termination of his previous temporary appointment.

In other words, any chance for promotion in the future was, in light of a "full review of circumstances leading up to the termination," unlikely. The language is polite compared to the dispatches leading up to his hearing where he was considered a detriment to the mission in Europe and totally lacking in decision making, ship control, and overall command ability. Polite, but direct and firm. There would be no reconsideration of the case. In fact, the only reconsideration would be in the event of an application for promotion where the entire incident would, more than likely, disqualify Caldin permanently.

Despite all of this, Caldin continued to serve. He returned humbly to his former rank and saw the same career trajectory he had forgotten. A world before the war. Before "90-day wonders." Before so much opportunity. Caldin needed the Navy and the Navy needed him. The U.S. Navy saw a force of 3.4 million in 1945 shrink to 484,000 by 1947. The "90-day wonders," the men who brought so much change, all went home. But the Caldins of the Navy remained.

Caldin spent the rest of the war filling out shore duties such as stevedore training out of Norfolk, VA. After the war, he served aboard several ships including the USS *Waccamaw* participating in the Suez Crisis in 1956. He retired shortly after and died two years later from a heart attack. Adnah Nyhart Caldin gave his life to the Navy and lived it the Navy way. Whether motivated to overcome his humble upbringing, to live up to the high standard of holding the namesake of one of the richest men in America, or simply because he had an extraordinary ambition to rise through the ranks as high as he could possibly go, Caldin stands as a byproduct of the American dream.

For every bootstrap story, for every American hero, for every unlikely kid who rises through the ranks to emerge a hero, there are many more who only achieve half their dreams. Captain Queeg was a cracked ego, a villain only redeemed by his loyalty to the Navy. But we know too much about Adnah Caldin. He was a complex person with a story that began from his childhood until the day he returned home to his family after the war.

1942   1943   1949

1954

Photos of Adnah Caldin, his wife Louis, and daughter Lucy.

Today, in Tidioute, Pennsylvania, the hotel where Adnah Caldin grew up still stands. It's now called the Hotel Tidioute and it gained a brief celebrity in 2010, when it was featured on the television show *American Pickers.* There's a plaque down the street that lists all of the local men and women who served in the armed forces from the small town that has grown even smaller over the years. Adnah Caldin's name is listed as a veteran of WWI but no mention is made of his service in WWII. If you cross the bridge heading south across the Allegheny River, and take a left you'll find an historical sign reading:

THE GRANDIN WELL

At an oil spring across the river, J. L. Grandin began the second well drilled specifically for oil in Aug 1859, after Drake's success. It was dry, showing the risks involved in oil drilling.

J. L. Grandin was an immensely wealthy and successful businessman who made his fortune in the oil industry. But history has flattened the divide between the Grandin and Caldin family. In the end, J. L. Grandin is remembered only for his failures and not his achievement. The success that Caldin was striving for most of his life has all but faded from his hometown and even from those who seemed poised, at one time, to lift him into greatness.

Afterward

Jim White sat in an officer's bar in New York City nursing a Tom Collins. He had bad reactions to the morphine that was supposed to help ease the pain from the severe fracture to his skull.

"I felt just like I was drowning all over again," he recalled. "A British doctor told me I was pretty messed up and I was going to need something to push through the pain."

Back in New York, when splitting headaches became unbearable, a Navy doctor told him to find an air-conditioned bar and have a drink or two. White, who never liked liquor or its effects, needed something to drown the pain before it drowned him.

But the physical pain wasn't all that tormented White. His ship was gone. Most of his men were dead or severely injured. And his once promising naval career was over. He asked the bartender if he could stay in the air conditioning for the afternoon. Eyeing Jim's severe head wound, the bartender poured him another drink.

"They're on the house," he said leaving, White alone again with his thoughts and his Tom Collins.

"I really felt things unravel for me then. And it took me a long time to put it all back together."

It's impossible to outline the lives of every single man who served aboard the *Partridge*. Reading the newsletters, most had families, became cops or fireman, businessmen, ranchers, and some had long careers in the Navy. A few served time in prison and some just seemed to have disappeared.

For Lt. Lefavor, a full military career of 33 years lay before him serving as an executive officer aboard numerous ships, ranging from oilers to minesweepers. The engineering officer seemed to have rescued his career after he emerged from the shadow of Caldin. He retired in 1967 and, like many men who devoted their lives to the Navy, died a few short years later.

Tom Buffum was discharged from the Navy shortly after the war ended. He returned to his home in Rhode Island, got a job in sales, and met a girl named Trudy. They were married in 1948. He eventually joined the family business importing jewelry and remained active in the Naval Reserve for most of the rest of his life.

Jim White did put things back together. He returned to California, got married, and became an optometrist in 1950, setting up a practice in Colton, California. Bill Ames encouraged everyone to stop in for a checkup if they were ever in town.

Mike Rich left active service in 1948 but continued in the reserves for many years to come. He eventually moved back to his hometown of Latrobe and married. He remained active in the Naval Reserve, eventually rising to the rank of lieutenant commander. He continued his education at the University of Colorado and retired as an executive at the Teledyne Vasco Corporation. Writing many years later to Patrick Cooney, who was just a child when his father died, Rich reflected his feelings about his cabin mate and friend:

"I liked your father and mourned for him. He was a good man and one I will never forget. I am sorry for the loss of your father defending his country."

Mike Rich returned to Normandy during his retirement, laying a wreath over the spot in the Channel where the *Partridge* went down. He passed away at the age of 92 on February 14, 2015.

Mike Rich laying a memorial in Normandy France.

Dalton Kirkman returned to his two daughters, who desperately clung to him. While home recovering, he met and married his second wife, Gaynelle Hill, on August 16, 1944, and reported for duty aboard the USS *Shelby,* which served in the Okinawa campaign and was attributed to the first gunnery action on a kamikaze that sunk another ship. After the war, he worked the family farm, fixed cars, started a career in law enforcement, and raised a large family. He died of Non-Hodgkin's lymphoma on January 11, 1984, survived by seven children and 14 grandchildren. My grandfather and Kirkman were close friends and wrote to each other often, but never saw each other after the *Partridge* sank.

Bud Froehlich, who recorded much of the *Partridge's* history in the Caribbean, went on to become an engineer on several Naval and private enterprises. He's widely credited with being the inventor of the Alvin submarine, which was used by Robert Ballard to explore the *Titanic*. He also engineered high-altitude balloons for Boeing. He credited the officers of the *Partridge* for mentoring him and encouraging him to continue his studies after the war.

Al Riker survived the sinking and recovered from his wounds. But shrapnel from the explosion that sank the *Partridge* remained in his leg. Later in life, the area around the metal in his leg began to bother him. In 1993 he went into surgery to correct the problem, but complications set in during the operation and he never woke up.

Joe and Betty Feeney stayed married and eventually had five children together. He remained a fireman in South Boston for 32 years, retiring as a lieutenant. He and Betty became passionate advocates for air quality in South Boston and were recognized by the American Lung Association for their efforts to compel Boston Edison to reduce power plant emissions. Feeney passed away from lung cancer in 1985.

After the war, Edward Janeway moved to Vermont and became a dairy farmer. He was elected to several local and state offices, and evenutally became a State Senator, serving 10 terms from 1959 to 1979.

Bob Miller, the UP report aboard the Partridge, went on to cover the liberation of France and the Nuremburg Trials. He covered stories all over the globe including the wars in Korea and Vietnam. He eventually settled as the head of the UPI Honolulu bureau. He passed away in Hawaii in 2014.

After Bill Ames was awarded the Purple Heart and received a discharge, he returned to Milwaukee and married his high school sweetheart Dotty and then graduated from the Milwaukee School of Engineering. He enjoyed a 48-year career in the design, manufacture, and application of industrial refrigeration systems. In addition to this, he was vice president of a livestock research company involving a large cattle-feeding operation and a string of racehorses.

Bill Ames receiving the Purple Heart from Captain Ceres at the Great Lakes Naval Hospital

Bill and Dotty Ames during our last in-person interview in 2007

Ames was one of the longest-serving men aboard the *Partridge* and became the glue that kept many of the men together for so long. He kept a newsletter running from 1948 until the early 50s and remained passionate about his time in the Navy and, in particular, his time aboard the *Partridge*. Bill and I spent many hours talking about the ship and her crew. He recounted past reunions and ideas for future ones, possibly returning to the Caribbean to visit some of his former ports of call. More than anything, Bill remembered the men he served with, recalling memories long forgotten as we would read through muster rolls pulled from the National Archives. When Bill passed away in November 2010, Joe Shannon wrote in an email:

"He is in God's hands now. He will probably tell God all about the *Partridge*. God will listen."

When my grandfather would tell me his war stories, they often focused on the night the ship was lost. It simply sank; vanished beneath the waves. My grandfather stepped off into the water and swam to a floating bridge until a Canadian ship rescued him and his fellow crew-members.

It was a version of the war for a child and didn't include the many horrors that contributed to his combat fatigue and years of screaming nightmares. Like many men of his generation, my grandfather preferred to leave his memories in the past. The Antietam Creek where we sailed homemade boats during summer visits had once flowed with blood after one of the most horrific battles of the Civil War. Now there were only toy boats and grandchildren. True memories of war are always muted, blunted, or altogether forgotten.

My grandfather died in 1988 after Alzheimer's disease robbed him of his ability to speak for almost eight years; our chance for an adult conversation about the war was never possible. Interviewing his shipmates and their families was a second chance at that conversation that I was lucky to have.

An unexpected result of researching this book has been finding the relatives of those who were killed when the ship sank. It seems every year a family will search the Internet for the *Partridge* and find my contact information on www.usspartridge.com. They have told me about grandmothers who were married before the war and had never told the family about first husbands killed in action. Or a long-lost brother, all but forgotten. Or a great-uncle whose name was a terminal branch on the family tree. For all of these families, the *Partridge* and her history were cut off by a telegram informing them that their loved one was dead or missing. The *Partridge* stories were passed on by the living but not to the families of the dead. It's been a great privilege to bring these two worlds together and shine light on forgotten or unknown personal histories.

As a seven-year-old, riding in the back of my grandparents' car driving one evening, I stared out at the darkened farmland, feeling my stomach rise and fall over the bumpy country road. It seemed like the perfect time to ask my grandfather to tell the story just one more time. About the night the ship sank and he swam toward the bridge in the middle of the water waiting to be rescued.

I didn't know it at the time, listening to him tell his war story, but there were people out in that dark night who yearned to hear it too. There was no one they knew to tell them about that night. For them, it was a missing part of their history; the story they were looking for was sunk somewhere deep in the ocean and far away.

Today, the *Partridge* lies on the bottom of the English Channel off Normandy. The ship was heavily salvaged in the late Forties and early Fifties. The crew joked at reunions that she probably ended up in more than a few Renaults and Peugeots. A museum in France houses her range finder, encased in rust. A flag supposedly taken from the *Partridge* before she sank exists in the Navy Historical Center in Norfolk. But this may be fanciful given how quickly the ship went down.

You can see a faint outline of the *Partridge's* shape in three-dimensional sonar renderings. Divers have explored her skeletal wreck covered in sea-life, some noting, incorrectly, that she went down without loss of life. Many pass over her as a mere footnote in a great battle that took place a long time ago. Nevertheless, she is the keeper of a human drama that transpired across her decks, within her cabins, her bridge, her engine room. Her profile is so faint now, her structure so crumbled, it is easy to believe that she and her crew were only a fiction.

But this tattered fragment of history was the beginning of a narrative that influenced how we view ourselves as Americans in war and in peace: how we lead and follow and how we live, fight, and die together. The crumbled Bird at the bottom of the channel and the growing list of obituaries from her crew is a reminder of how fragile history is beyond written words on a page. She is a Bird sunk deep in the ocean, but not deep enough for her to be completely out of reach.

Jim White had heard once about an historic low tide in the English Channel and dreamed of walking in knee-deep water, retracing his journey toward France.

"I would have liked to go back there," he said, imagining the channel nearly drained. "I would have liked to walk out there and find my ship."

The Partridge's range finder recovered from her wreck off the coast of Normandy. Photo: Mike Rich

Acknowledgments

I would like to thank all of the people who made this book possible. The veterans of the Partridge whom, I had the privilege to interview over countless hours, offered invaluable perspective on this story. Sadly, most of them did not live long enough to see this book published. Still I am forever in debt to Bill and Dotty Ames, Mike Rich, Joe Shannon, Robert Ainslie, Floyd Pedersen, and many others for sharing their memories, diaries, and photographs from their time aboard the ship. Also thank you to family and friends of the crew including Betty Eide, Annie Mix, Patrick Cooney, Mary Neale, Tom Buffum, Jr., Dorothy Lamb, Lisa Knott, Shannon Donovan, and Lucy Wagenaar. I am also thankful to my grandmother, Doris Krouse, who kept meticulous scrapbooks from the era that prove not everything is preserved on the Internet.

To staff and researchers at the National Archives: thank you for all that you do. It's amazing work that goes on tirelessly and the care and compassion you bring to someone else's project is amazing. I only wish I could have spent more time in College Park.

I would also like to thank my family for their love and support throughout this long project. Especially my wife who has followed this dream through many more years than I originally promised. Finally, I would like to thank my father, John Krouse, whose curiosity and passion for this project have helped me see it through to publication. You'll always be an inspiration for me.

About the Author

James Krouse is an author and playwright. He lives in Cleveland Heights, Ohio, with his wife and two children.

CPSIA information can be obtained
at www.ICGtesting.com
Printed in the USA
BVHW061927071019
560431BV00003B/37/P